DEDICATED TO GANDALF
SERVANT OF THE SECRET FIRE

The Lord of the Rings Tarot
Editor: Nancy Martsch

Library of Congress Cataloging-in-Publication Data

Donaldson, Terry.
    The Lord of the rings tarot / by Terry Donaldson. -- 1st ed.
        p.   cm.
    Includes bibliographical references.
    ISBN 1-57281-054-8
    1. Tarot. 2. Tolkien, J. R. R. (John Ronald Reuel), 1892-1973.
Lord of the Rings. I. Title.
BF1879.T2D64 1997
133.3'2424--dc21

99 10 9 8 7 6 5 4 3 2

Printed in Canada

U.S. Games Systems, Inc.
179 Ludlow Street
Stamford, CT 06902 USA

THE LORD OF THE RINGS TAROT

The Lord of the Rings Tarot

by Terry Donaldson

U.S. GAMES
SYSTEMS, INC

U.S. GAMES SYSTEMS, INC.
Publishers
179 Ludlow Street
Stamford, CT 06902 U.S.A.

Contents

Acknowledgments

These are the people who have contributed to the creation of this classic tarot deck. They each know their respective contributions. Many thanks are due for their efforts and contributions, friendship and support:

Evelyne and Claudia Donaldson, Sammy and Jane Wilcox, Tina Slade, Fiona and Freya Brown, Jazz Deville, Shelly Pink, Lou Gallant, Ian Percival, Rebecca Pracownik, Vicky Miller, Kathryn Eyre, Janet Moorey, Michelle Pilley, Susan Mears, and Des J. Simmonds.

An especial *thank you* to Laurie Battle of Tolkien Enterprises for her support, advice, and personal enthusiasm for this project.

I
Welcome to Middle-earth

It has been said that the world is divided into two categories: those who have read *The Lord of the Rings*, and those who have yet to read it. In *The Lord of the Rings*, J. R. R. Tolkien has seemingly brought together elements of the legends of many cultures over a very long period of history into a single story—his own original mythology.

The Lord of the Rings is clearly one of the greatest publishing success stories of the century, and interest in the mythic world of Tolkien is constantly increasing throughout the world. *The Lord of the Rings* has been published in over twenty languages, and has sold millions of copies. There has also been a considerable spin-off industry—Tolkien trinkets and souvenirs, T-shirts, maps, calendars, posters, bestiaries, films, *ad infinitum*.

John Ronald Reuel Tolkien was born on January 3, 1892, in Bloemfontein, South Africa, the elder of the two sons of Arthur and Mabel Tolkien. This young couple from Birmingham, England, had traveled to the dusty plains of South Africa where Arthur Tolkien was to manage a bank. When Ronald (as Tolkien was called) was three years old, his mother returned to visit England with the two children; and while they were away, Arthur Tolkien died.

Tolkien's memories of South Africa were scant, although he did remember being bitten by a tarantula. Some have suggested that the experience with the spider must have been profound, looking at the role which spiders play in Mirkwood and again at Shelob's Lair; but Tolkien always maintained this wasn't so.

Mabel Tolkien never remarried. At first she taught her sons at home; later they were sent to school, where they studied Latin and other standard subjects of the time. Here young Ronald discovered the Old English language (Anglo-Saxon), which was to be the love of his life. He had a genius for language. Mabel Tolkien converted to Roman Catholicism, and was ostracized by her Protestant family. She died of diabetes when Ronald was twelve. The Tolkien brothers' guardian was Father Francis Morgan, a Catholic priest. The Christian faith remained a deep source of spiritual consolation for Tolkien all of his life. He lived in various homes with his brother Hilary, studied at King Edward's school in Birmingham, and continued to thrive in his study of languages and mythology. When he was sixteen he met Edith Bratt, an orphan boarding in the same house as Tolkien, but he was forbidden by Father Morgan to court her. They had to wait until Tolkien turned twenty-one.

Tolkien earned a scholarship to Oxford University, where he studied philology and English. World War I broke out: upon completing his studies, Tolkien married his sweetheart Edith, was sent to France, and fought in the Battle of the Somme. He became ill with trench fever, and while recuperating in the hospital he began to write down the myths and legends which would eventually become *The Silmarillion* and provide the background for *The Lord of the Rings*.

After the war ended, Tolkien became a Professor of Anglo-Saxon and English Literature, first at Leeds University (1920-1925) and then at Oxford University, where he would remain from 1925 to his retirement in 1959. Tolkien had a special interest in the Finnish Kalevala and the Icelandic and Norse legends of giants, gods, and demons. He and a group of friends, of whom the writers C. S. Lewis and Charles Williams were most prominent, formed a club they called "The Inklings" that convened to talk and read aloud from the members' works.

One day Tolkien scribbled on the back of an examination paper, "In a hole in the ground there lived a hobbit." He could not say what hobbits were or where they came from. (Since then people have found hobbit-type names in various places.) He simply hit upon a name, and then had to figure out the story around it. This particular story, first read to his children (the Tolkiens had three sons and a daughter), became *The Hobbit*.

Sir Stanley Unwin, the original publisher of *The Hobbit*, gave Tolkien's manuscript to his ten-year-old son Rayner to be reviewed. Unwin reasoned that if his son liked it, he would publish it. Rayner gave it a rave review, and so it went to print. *The Hobbit* was published in September 1937; the first edition was sold out by Christmas. The American edition was issued a few months later and was awarded *The New York Herald Tribune* prize for the best juvenile book of the season. Unwin sensed that a sequel to *The Hobbit* would also sell. Meeting with Tolkien a few weeks after *The Hobbit* had been published, Unwin learned that the professor did in fact have other material: a tremendous mythological work called *The Silmarillion*, which describes the origins of the universe and the stories of the gods and goddesses leading up to the events with which most of us are familiar in *The Lord of the Rings*.

Tolkien felt quite strongly about the importance of *The Silmarillion*, for it depicts the early history of Elves and Men as they struggled through the Elder Days and the collapse of Númenor (Atlantis). One may find contained within *The Silmarillion* the secrets of how we can effectively guide humanity in its evolution onto its next phase. But Unwin was more interested in Tolkien producing a sequel to *The Hobbit*, so Tolkien began *The Lord of the Rings*. There were many times when Tolkien felt like giving up on the project; but he didn't, and in between tutorials for his students he wrote out the entire story, much of it by hand. Unwin and Tolkien's friend, C. S. Lewis, offered encouragement over the next twelve and a half years until the manuscript for *The Lord of the Rings* was finally completed.

Tolkien still wanted to publish *The Silmarillion* as well, although it was unfinished. He broke away from Unwin in an attempt to get both *The Silmarillion* and *The Lord of the Rings* published by Collins, another London publishing house, in one composite volume; but this never came to pass, so Tolkien returned to Unwin and agreed to the publication of *The Lord of the Rings* on its own in three volumes.

The first volume of *The Lord of the Rings*, *The Fellowship of the Ring*, was published in England in July 1954, and in the United States in October 1954. The second volume, *The Two Towers*, came out in England in November 1954, and in the United States in April 1955. Volume three, *The Return of the King*, appeared in England in October 1955, and in the United States in January 1956.

Sadly, Tolkien did not live to see the publication, nor even the completion, of *The Silmarillion*. His son, Christopher, undertook the monumental task of editing the work, and it was published in 1977.

The Storyline

The story begins in *The Hobbit*.

Bilbo Baggins is a Hobbit, living a comfortable, quiet, safe life in the Shire, when Gandalf, a wizard, calls upon him. The next day, Gandalf and thirteen Dwarves, by ones and by twos, turn up at Bilbo's door. The Dwarves take over his home, announcing that they are pleased to have someone like Bilbo in their company. They are about to undertake a hazardous expedition to recover their ancestral treasure from Smaug the dragon. We later discover that upon leaving Bilbo's home the first time, Gandalf had marked Bilbo's door with a sign announcing a professional burglar in residence, available for work.

Bilbo finds himself swept away into this adventure with the Dwarves, in which they are captured by (and escape from) Trolls, Goblins, spiders, and Elves at different points in their journey. In the caves under the mountains Bilbo becomes separated from his companions. At an underground lake he meets Gollum, a predatory-type character who engages him in a riddle contest. Bilbo, unbeknownst to Gollum, has just found a ring which he has slipped into his pocket, and which—so it transpires—is the property of this creature. When Gollum realizes his loss, Bilbo runs away. He quickly discovers (to his amazement) that he has placed the ring on his finger, and that it has made him invisible. And so he escapes from the underground cave.

Rejoining his group, they arrive (after many adventures) at the Lonely Mountain, where the great dragon Smaug has a vast treasure hoard containing, among other jewels, the precious Arkenstone. Bilbo is sent to check out Smaug's cave, and inadvertently provokes the dragon into making an attack on a nearby town. As it does so, Smaug is shot down by Bard the Bowman, who has learned of a soft spot in the dragon's underbelly. Smaug dies, and immediately various other interested parties begin marching on the mountain in order to be the first to loot the treasure for themselves. Elves and Men besiege the mountain, with Bilbo's group of Dwarves inside—secure from attack, but totally trapped within. Both the besiegers, as well as Bilbo's by-now fanatical Dwarf companions, are unable to find any compromise. To break the stalemate, Bilbo takes the Arkenstone, creeps out of the mountain whilst wearing the ring, and places the Arkenstone in the hands of the besiegers. A compromise is attained; but before it can be implemented, more Dwarves, Goblins, and wolves arrive. The Dwarves unite with Men and Elves against the Goblins and wolves. Men, Elves, and Dwarves come together to fight the forces of negativity who have come to try to steal the dragon's treasure for themselves. Afterwards, Bilbo returns to his native land—the Shire—taking with him the mysterious ring (and a mail shirt and magic sword).

The story continues with *The Lord of the Rings*. It's Bilbo's 111th birthday, and he is going on a journey. He plans to leave in a spectacular fashion: vanishing in front of the people he has invited to his birthday party by putting on the Ring. Yet Gandalf has to remind Bilbo of his promise to leave the Ring behind. Bilbo leaves the Ring, along with all of his other possessions, to Frodo Baggins, his nephew. Time passes, and a number of years later Gandalf returns to inform Frodo that the Ring has strange powers which are likely to corrupt anyone who wears and makes use of it. He reveals that Sauron, the Dark Lord who made the Ring, is looking for his Ring, and that Frodo is in danger. Frodo makes plans to take the Ring out of the Shire and go to

Rivendell, home of Elrond Half-elven.

Frodo will be accompanied by Sam Gamgee, his gardener, who knows about the Ring. Frodo sells his home (Bag End), ostensibly to move to another home near the border of the Shire. The night they are to leave, Frodo overhears a stranger asking Sam's father about "Baggins." Frodo, Sam, and Pippin (Frodo's cousin) depart, taking a little-used road. Along the way, they hear hoof-beats behind them, and, filled with fear, they hide out. Frodo feels strangely tempted to put on the Ring. The horseman is not a Hobbit farmer, as expected, but a big Man cloaked in black, riding a black horse—the stranger who had asked for "Baggins"! The pursuit has begun.

That night the Hobbits are saved from the Black Rider by the timely arrival of a group of Elves. Next they attempt a shortcut and wind up on the fields of Farmer Maggot. All his life, Frodo had been afraid of Maggot and his dogs; now he finds that the farmer is a friend. Finally, they arrive at Frodo's new home, where his cousin Merry awaits them. (Both Merry and Pippin, unbeknownst to Frodo, know about the Ring.)

To throw off the pursuit of the Black Rider, they attempt another shortcut through the Old Forest, a place of ill-repute beyond the border of the Shire. There they are trapped by an evil tree, Old Man Willow, and rescued by Tom Bombadil, a sort of nature spirit. They spend a day at Tom's house.

In order to return to the road, the Hobbits must cross the Barrow-downs, a place of ancient tombs (barrows) haunted by evil spirits (Barrow-wights). They are caught, and Frodo cuts off the Barrow-wight's hand. Tom rescues them again, and they arm themselves with swords from the barrow.

At length they reach the Prancing Pony Inn at Bree. During

the evening's festivities, Frodo either accidentally or just plain unwisely slips on the Ring and vanishes from the sight of the other merrymakers. An uproar ensues, although they are able to smooth the situation over; and they meet with a rough-looking man called Strider (Aragorn). He offers his assistance, which the travelers accept, though not without much doubt and trepidation at first. Aragorn's advice enables them to avoid an attack on the Inn by the Black Riders, and they escape off the main road in the direction of Rivendell. En route, the Black Riders attack again, and their Captain wounds Frodo with a poisoned Morgul blade, which turns its victim into a wraith. Resisting the evil spell of the Riders, Frodo makes it to the ford of the Loudwater near Rivendell. As the Riders begin to cross the waters, a great wave washes them away, drowning their horses and breaking up their attack.

At Rivendell Elrond heals Frodo's wound. They meet Bilbo, who is residing there, writing his memoirs. He gives his mail shirt and sword to Frodo, and a Great Council is held to decide what to do with this Ring that seems to be causing so much trouble. The Ring is a powerful artifact for evil, originally made by Sauron, the Dark Lord of Mordor, and contains a vast amount of his energy. The idea of using this Ring against the Dark Lord and his increasingly aggressive army of Orcs (Goblins) in the east is voiced, and overruled—for anyone who uses the Ring to dominate others will become evil. Besides, using the Ring for personal gain is precisely the kind of move which Sauron would expect them to make. The Ring, it is agreed, will have to be destroyed, and this can only be done by throwing it into the fires of Mount Doom, the volcano where the Ring was originally made, in the land of Mordor. Frodo volunteers to destroy the Ring. Elrond chooses Nine Companions to achieve this quest: Nine Companions against the Nine Black Riders of Mordor. All races will be represented: the Hobbits by Frodo and Sam, and Merry and Pippin; Aragorn and Boromir for Mortal Men; Legolas for the Elves; Gimli for the Dwarves; and the wizard Gandalf.

They set off. En route, the Companions have to change course, as they cannot cross the great Misty Mountains in the snow, and they are in danger. They decide to go through Moria, a labyrinth of old mines created by the Dwarves long before, the only way that they can continue on their quest. They almost make it through the mines, when they are attacked by Orcs and a Balrog, a monster with a whip of fire. Gandalf battles this creature, and both fall into an abyss.

They have crossed under the Misty Mountains, but they have lost Gandalf. In the hidden Elven land of Lothlórien, the Companions are comforted in their grief, and are given advice and gifts by the Elven Lady Galadriel and her husband, Lord Celeborn. The Elves also give them boats to continue their journey down the Great River Anduin, until they can go no further this way. Boromir attempts to persuade Frodo to come with him to his city of Minas Tirith; then tries to take the Ring by force. Frodo puts on the Ring, becomes invisible, and escapes.

Frodo and Sam slip off toward Mordor. Pippin and Merry run into a band of Orcs, and are captured. Boromir dies trying to defend them. At this point the two groups move in different directions—Sam and Frodo travel into Mordor, while Aragorn, Gimli, and Legolas try and rescue Pippin and Merry. The Orc raiding party, meanwhile, is surrounded by the horsemen of Rohan, and during the ensuing battle, both of the Hobbits are able to escape. Pippin and Merry flee into the forest and arouse the Ents, the shepherds of the trees, who are angry at the Orcs for cutting their trees. (This raiding party was composed of Orcs from Mordor and Orcs from the wizard Saruman in Orthanc. Saruman, the head of the Order of Wizards, has turned traitor.) The Ents march on Orthanc.

Meanwhile, Frodo and Sam make their slow way toward Mordor. They capture Gollum, who has been following them ever since Moria (remember, he wants his Ring back). Frodo makes him swear an oath of allegiance on the Ring to lead them to Mordor, for Gollum knows the way. Unfortunately, Gollum attempts a betrayal, and leads them into the lair of Shelob, a giant spider-like demon. Frodo drives off Shelob with the light of the small Phial of starlight given to him by Galadriel. Gollum attacks, and Shelob stings Frodo. Sam rescues his master, injuring the monster with Frodo's magic sword, but too late: Frodo is dead. Weeping, Sam takes the Ring to continue the journey to Mount Doom. Orc patrols approach; Sam slips on the Ring and becomes invisible. The Orcs discover the body of Frodo, and from their talk Sam learns that Frodo is not dead after all, only paralyzed—but a prisoner of the Orcs! They take him into their watchtower; Sam bravely uses the Phial to enter and rescues Frodo. Disguising themselves as Orcs, the two Companions continue on toward Mount Doom.

At the same time, in the land of Rohan, Aragorn, Legolas, and Gimli are pursuing the Orc raiders. They meet Gandalf, now Gandalf the White, returned from the dead to counteract Sauron. He informs them the Ents have Pippin and Merry, and they must go to the King of Rohan. Gandalf meets with old King Théoden, and frees him from the hypnotic spell of his evil counselor Gríma Wormtongue. Théoden realizes that instead of caving in to the power of Saruman, Rohan's neighbor, they must fight. Théoden's men encounter Saruman's army, and take refuge in the stronghold of Helm's Deep. King Théoden leads a brave charge which panics the Orcs into retreating; Gandalf arrives with reinforcements, and they are saved. The Ents have destroyed Orthanc, and the Hobbits and other Companions are briefly reunited.

Gandalf's priority now is to ensure the safety of the city of Minas Tirith, capital of Gondor, for across the Great River lies Mordor. Gandalf and Pippin ride to Minas Tirith. Aragorn, Legolas, and Gimli take the Paths of the Dead, an ancient passage under the mountains, haunted by the ghosts of warriors who had broken an oath to Aragorn's ancestor. Aragorn summons the Oathbreakers to his aid, and the Army of the Dead routs Sauron's attack in the south. King Théoden rides to the aid of Minas Tirith, and with him are his niece Éowyn (in disguise) and Merry. The Rohirrim arrive in the nick of time, Théoden is killed, and Éowyn, assisted by Merry, kills the Witch-king, the Captain of the Black Riders.

Minas Tirith is saved. The armies regroup, and attack Mordor—to draw the attention of Sauron away from Frodo. Frodo and Sam make it to Mt. Doom, but Frodo cannot destroy the Ring: its hold on him has grown too strong. Gollum tries to take the Ring from Frodo, bites off Frodo's finger (with the Ring on it), and falls into the volcano's fires. And so the Ring is destroyed. The power of Sauron collapses, the flying Black Riders disintegrate, and Frodo and Sam are rescued.

Aragorn is crowned King of Gondor and marries Arwen, daughter of Elrond. But Saruman has left Orthanc and is headed for the Shire, bent on revenge. When the four Hobbits return home, they find great destruction. They rouse the Shire, there is a fight, Saruman dies, and the War of the Rings comes to an end. Elrond, Galadriel, Gandalf, Bilbo, and Frodo set sail for the Undying Lands beyond the West, leaving Sam, Pippin, and Merry behind.

The Setting

Middle-earth, the setting for most of the epic, is a minutely mapped realm, geographically consistent, and dotted with colonies of inhabitation. The different kingdoms are occupied by vastly different civilizations, varying from the harsh brutal world of the Orcs in the eastern realm of Mordor to the simple Shire of the Hobbits, which is reminiscent of Oxfordshire or the Midlands, where Tolkien lived.

The three main spheres in Arda (the world) are Middle-earth, Númenor (Atlantis), and the Blessed Realm (Undying Lands)—although by the time of the War of the Ring these last two were no longer physically part of Arda. There are references to the collapse of the island continent Númenor, which fell into the sea; the final scene of *The Lord of the Rings* involves the departure of some of the main protagonists toward the Blessed Realm where gods and immortals dwell. Those who have left their homelands in search of freedom and civil rights may well feel a sense of kinship with these characters.

The scenery in which the action takes place in the stories has varying roles. Sometimes it is used to challenge a hero, or to house a demon or dark spirit. Following our protagonists on their journeys, we travel through mountains, lakes, subterranean passages, forests, marshes, and palaces.

The Characters

The search for Tolkien's sources takes us into the early literature of Iceland, Germany, Finland, and Celtic Europe. Aragorn fulfills the role of the king without a crown: he is of noble lineage, goes through many struggles, and eventually emerges victorious. He is crowned as the rightful king, and marries his beloved, the Lady Arwen. There are some parallels with the tales of both Arthur and Siegfried (and Jesus). A sword—which has a special history or powers associated with it—is in Aragorn's possession. Arthur took the sword from the stone, while Siegfried reforged his and then killed the dragon Fafnir, who had in his possession the powerful Ring of the Nibelungs. In the Arthurian stories there is no Ring; instead there is the Grail, which, like the Ring, is a feminine symbol. These are archetypal stories of the male who goes through various initiations in search of fulfillment that is only possible through the attainment of the feminine.

Gandalf fulfills a Merlin-type role, coming down from the astral plane to incarnate along with Saruman and three other brethren of the Istari, and assist the Free Peoples of Middle-earth against the Dark Lord. Alone amongst his brethren, he remains constant in his active opposition to the machinations of Sauron. This also makes him analogous in some ways to Christ. (Who, after he descends to this earth, then descends again into the underworld, from which he later rises.)

Galadriel and the Lady Éowyn fulfill two different feminine roles: the former as the wise woman who has access to mystical powers; the latter as a woman of action, decisive and assertive even in the face of danger. As archetypes or roles, they indicate the feminine within us all, men as well as women.

Saruman represents the corruption in high places which afflicts our societies, with people in positions of power with their secret agendas, for which the sacrifice of innocent people's rights or interests is a small price to pay. This corruption can exist in either high or low places in any society. Inwardly, Saruman represents our compromises with reality, leading us to lose sight of our long-term goals. As a symbol, he warns against self-aggrandizement: through his abandonment of his duties and responsibilities, he challenges us toward fulfillment of our own.

Ultimately, *The Lord of the Rings* is a story about how little people are able to overcome the immensely powerful forces of negativity, the tremendous challenges that spring up. Hobbits are shown as friendly, homey creatures who become heroes almost accidentally. The Free Peoples—Hobbits, Men, Elves, Dwarves—through tenacity, courage, loyalty, and ingenuity are successful in defending themselves against the massive armies of Orcs, who are directed by evil intelligences with vast magical abilities. Orcs epitomize evil, although Tolkien shows some humor in portraying their in-fighting.

There are two places where the dead are encountered in the story. One is where Gollum leads Frodo and Sam through the Dead Marshes on the way toward Mordor, and the other is where the spirits of the Oathbreakers are summoned by Aragorn to come to the aid of his forces and thus fulfill their oaths. In the former, the faces of the dead, seen submerged beneath the slimy surface, were not those of actual corpses, but an illusion, perhaps created by the enemy. Those who followed the "tricksy lights" that hovered above the marshy waters could be led to their deaths. It has long been believed that spirits produced such lights; this idea extends throughout many different bodies of folklore. One wonders if such souls were under the enchantment of Sauron, and were unable to rest until his destruction.

Tolkien was a devout Christian, although he had knowledge of other forms of symbolism. Those who read his works feel connected with a spiritual revelation, a new vision of how we can look upon symbolism and mythology. His stated purpose in writing *The Lord of the Rings* was to tell a good story. He did not aim to give spiritual instruction via allegory, nor to conceal hidden messages for the select. Nevertheless, his world of Middle-earth was peopled with supernatural beings, because unlike most other fantasy writers Tolkien had a profound knowledge of mythology, and brought in many unconscious references to the old gods and ancient archetypes held deeply within the human mind. One can read *The Lord of the Rings* as a *Pilgrim's Progress*-style rite of passage, showing how a group of souls goes through certain stages of initiations in overcoming various obstacles. As they fight and progress to the next level, they come to understand more about themselves and each other. The bonds which tie them together are strengthened, not weakened, through their repeated trials and tribulations. We have the experience of the Mines of Moria, a labyrinth symbol at the center of which lies a confrontation with the monster—the Minotaur—or in this case, the Balrog. We have the archetype of Satan, in the personage of Sauron the Dark Lord, a brooding malevolent force who we never actually get to see, but who remains in shadowy form throughout. Tolkien took the name "Orc" from the Old English *orc*, "demon," which may derive from the Latin *Orcus*, a Roman underworld deity: Orcs are reflections of the "demons" which trouble mankind (in our dimension, these demons include war, pestilence, violence, abuse, etc.). *Orc* is also the Irish word for "pig."

Tolkien made use of various animals in his story; for example, he writes of the white horses in the foam of the waves which sweep away the Nine Riders at the ford of the Loudwater. Horses have a great association in mythology. Odin was supposed to have ridden an eight-legged horse, Sleipnir (meaning "slippery"), a tall, white, magical steed that resembles Gandalf's great grey horse Shadowfax. In ancient British myth, such horses were sacred to the sun and the sea. Gandalf's arrival by sea from the West, and his subsequent departure back to the Blessed Realm after two thousand years in Middle-earth, conjures up all the tales of savior-gods throughout the world's mythology. In the theme of a journey, *The Lord of the Rings* parallels both Odysseus (Ulysses) and the Grail quest.

The Elves, according to Tolkien, were intended by Ilúvatar (God) to be the Firstborn. They were immortal, not subject to age or sickness (though their bodies could be slain or they might die of grief), tall and more beautiful than mortal humans; sometimes helpful toward humanity, sometimes hostile. They were fearsome as warriors, cunning and clever. Tolkien's Elves most resemble the Irish Sidhe, who were the remnants of the Tuatha Dé Danaan—the old gods of Ireland, diminished, but still retaining their earthly powers. The three most important characters from amongst the Elves are Galadriel, Elrond Half-elven, and Legolas.

Greek mythology holds many accounts of two races uniting and producing offspring. Hercules was born from the union of Zeus and a mortal woman. Elrond is descended from Elves and Men. On the negative side, terrible creatures such as the

Gorgons and the Scylla resulted from the union of gods and demons, or demons and humans. Saruman bred Orcs and Men to make Half-orcs.

The story of Half-elven Lady Arwen (daughter of Elrond Half-elven and Celebrían, daughter of Galadriel) and the mortal Man Aragorn is another such story showing the union of two races. One theme of this type of folklore is that such marriages seldom, if ever, come to any good. The mortal man is generally left in a negative situation at the end of the tale, when the woman goes back to her own people, or runs off, or shape-changes back into some other creature. But of the few unions between Elves and Men in Middle-earth, most came to good.

The Dwarves of Middle-earth were short, stocky, subterranean people who were very skilled in the working of stone and metal. In Teutonic myth, they lived in mountain ranges and caverns, not actually within the earth itself. While the Elves were attuned to nature, the Dwarves were smiths. In ancient Europe, metalwork was the prerogative of the shaman. Smiths were particularly revered by the Celts, and credited with having supernatural powers. In Norse mythology, the goddess Freyja was indebted to Dwarves for the creation of her golden necklace. It was Dwarves who also produced the magic bond for the wolf Fenris; it was made of six impossible things, including the breath of a fish and the sound of a cat running. The Dwarves of Tolkien's Middle-earth lived to a great old age, although their population rate had declined by the Third Age; there were few Dwarf women.

Tom Bombadil is a Pan/nature god figure, but Tolkien made him a more humorous (and chaste!) character. His divinity is seen in the fact that he was one the first spirits to inhabit Middle-earth. He was master of plant and animal life inside a circumscribed area including the Old Forest and the Barrow-downs. He was unfazed by natural or supernatural danger. Tolkien repeatedly emphasizes that Tom was his own master, and master of his surrounding lands—although not the owner of them. Even the Ring had no influence over him. His power lay in his gaiety and his sung spells. His wife, Goldberry, was a watersprite who sang about the beauty of nature.

The Ents were guardians of the woods, who hated tree cutters. They resemble the ancient fallen race of wise and faithful Giants, who were considered to be the oldest of all creatures; indeed, the name "Ent" derives from an Old English word for "giant." The Entwives cherished domestic plants and taught men their uses, rather like Demeter and Ceres, who gave the human race the gifts of agriculture and herbalism. But they went their separate ways; and the Ents mourned their lost Entwives.

Sauron personifies destruction and negativity: in pre-Christian myth, he corresponds with Loki, the trickster who eventually ends his association with the other gods and joins the side of the challenging demons. Our concept of dualism, the eternal battle between good and evil, may have originated from Persian Zendic concepts prevailing in the Near East, and is most fully developed in the form of Satan in Christian parlance. In *The Lord of the Rings*, Sauron had supernatural powers with regard to storms, the dead, and magical warfare. In non-Christian mythology, though, Sauron is most like Odin. One of Odin's titles was in fact Baleyg, or "Flame-eyed." Sauron poured his own personal spirit into the creation of the Ring, which he was never able to regenerate after the Ring was destroyed. It is a widespread belief among tribal peoples that the life force or soul can leave the physical body and be confined within an external object in the same way that Sauron put his into the Ring. Even to this day, some people are afraid of having their soul or life force charmed away, and shy away from photographs, or forbid the pictorial representation of people in their art.

The Nine Black Riders, or Nazgûl ("Ringwraiths"), were the most effective opposition to the Company of the Ring. They had once worn the Nine Rings and were now totally tied to Sauron. These Nine Rings were given to kings and lords (some of Númenórean descent) as a promise of power and immortality—instead, they brought enslavement. The Nazgûl were invisible (wraiths); they could only be fully seen by someone wearing the Ring, or by someone with supernatural power—but then, that person would be visible to them. They wore cloaks to give themselves shape when they went among Men. They projected an aura of fear. In the end, they were destroyed when the Ring was destroyed in Mount Doom.

The Trolls were less intelligent, although they possessed great strength. In Norway on St. John's Eve (Midsummer's Eve), bonfires of nine kinds of wood are burnt, along with toadstools, at crossroads. These fires are meant to overcome the power of the Trolls, who, if they are in the vicinity, are supposed to show themselves. Mistletoe is hung in barns to prevent Trolls from harming humans or animals.

The Orcs were created as a parody of the Elves by Morgoth the Great Enemy, Sauron's former master. In his dungeon fortress, Morgoth was said to have experimented with captured

Elves in order to produce Orcs. Morgoth was one of the Valar (gods) who turned to evil: he is most closely analogous to the Christian Lucifer. Although Morgoth was expelled from the world long ago, his evil lives on. Orcs can make no beautiful things, but they are clever and wicked; and their only fulfillment in life is to destroy and kill, which made them useful to Morgoth and Sauron as fighters.

Contrasting with these creatures, the Balrog was a vast elemental force which was able to rival even Gandalf, and that whilst he was wearing his Ring of Fire. The Balrogs—as a race—were originally spirits who became evil through their service to Morgoth. The Balrog resembles the Norse Surt or a Christian devil; each was a huge figure combining darkness with a consuming fire. Each was armed with a flaming sword and fought on a high frail bridge, breaking it down.

With the destruction of Sauron, most of the Wise traveled toward the Undying Lands, and Middle-earth entered into a New Age under the dominion of Mankind. In just the same way, after Ragnarök, the earth rose cleansed from the sea, still crowned by the great World Ash Yggdrasil, and sheltered mortal man and woman in its branches.

In Tolkien's world, dragons are shown in their most negative light, being totally greedy and aggressive. The dragon Smaug occupies a central place in *The Hobbit*, although he doesn't appear in *The Lord of the Rings*. (Nor does any other dragon, for that matter.) Whereas in the East, dragons are considered to be good luck, in Europe they quickly became associated with serpents, and therefore with something that could strike out and kill you—or at least injure you—with no prior warning at all. In Christian mythology, the dragon is a symbol of evil.

Wagner's version of Norse mythology tells the story of Siegfried, who reforges his father's sword and goes off to kill Fafnir the dragon, a giant who had transformed himself into a dragon in order to guard the Nibelung Ring and treasure hoard. We also have the fierce battle between Thor and the World Serpent Jormungand, whose body encircled the world. Thor dies in this battle, a familiar theme affecting heroes throughout mythology. And Grendel, the dragon in *Beowulf*, was a direct inspiration for Smaug in *The Hobbit*.

The theme of magic rings is very important in Tolkien's realm, as with world mythology in general. The ancients held that even ordinary rings were powerful talismans, which was why gypsies and fortune tellers tended to wear many of them. Scandinavian and Anglo-Saxon kings demonstrated their generosity by giving away rings, usually arm-rings, to their deserving followers. Some mythological rings were said to enable the wearer to change shape. In the Arthurian cycle, Sir Gareth is given a ring which disguises him at a tournament by changing his colors. In Teutonic folklore, the primary purpose of any ring was to increase wealth. Odin's ring had this effect. Often the ring is cursed, as it was—twice—in Wagner's version of the Nibelung Ring. It was supposed to bring initial benefits, but then corruption, until finally its wearer would be overtaken by tragedy. Murder and treachery run throughout Wagner's tale of what happened to each of the Ring's owners—brother would turn against brother without a second thought. Fafnir killed his brother Fasolt by hitting him in the back of the head, and then picked up the Ring along with the rest of the treasure the two took from Wotan (Odin) in payment for having built Valhalla. The gods stood by, shocked, as Fafnir calmly picked up the gold and strode off, leaving his brother dead in front of them.

The Three Elven Rings had stones colored red, white, and blue—respectively, Gandalf's Ring epitomized fire; Galadriel's, water; and Elrond's, air (blue sky for air). The missing element is earth. Tolkien doesn't say so outright, but the One Ring might well represent this element (i.e., mastery over the physical plane).

The weapons used in the story are another aspect to which Tolkien paid great attention. Both Bilbo's sword Sting and Farmer Giles's sword Tailbiter (in Tolkien's story *Farmer Giles of Ham*) were magical in that they gave advance warning of the approach of any enemy. Sting, Gandalf's sword Glamdring, and Thorin's blade Orcrist each glowed with a mysterious light when Orcs were nearby. By the intensity of the glow, they could tell how many the Orcs numbered, and how far away they were. If any dragon came within five miles, Farmer Giles's sword would jump out of its sheath. In Rohan, the important weapons were Éomer's sword Gúthwinë and Théoden's sword Herugrim. The most important sword of all was Andúril, belonging to Aragorn. This sword broke under the weight of King Elendil's body when he was slain by Sauron, but his son Isildur used it to cut the Ring from Sauron's hand. The Elves of Rivendell reforged it for Aragorn, a familiar theme in both the Arthurian mysteries and the Germanic Volsungsaga. The name Andúril means "Flame of the West." Galadriel gave Aragorn a sheath for Andúril, which also possessed special powers to protect the sword. Excalibur's sheath was supposed to be even more powerful than the blade itself, to the effect that as long as Arthur wore the scabbard, he would not lose blood, no matter how badly he might be wounded.

In *The Lord of the Rings,* we encounter just about every possible human experience and emotion: love, loyalty, treachery, fear, bravery, compassion, complexity, straightforwardness. The beings that live in Middle-earth are as varied as the lands they inhabit. In almost all cases, Tolkien has given the impression that he has told much less than he knows about the people in question, rather than just having produced random lineage to fill up space. The Dúnedain ("Men of the West") are the descendants of the Númenóreans (Atlanteans). Humanity is portrayed as coming into its own—the Age of Men is approaching, while that of the Third Age was receding.

II
The Significance of Tolkien's Genius

J. R. R. Tolkien loved trees. He loved to walk amongst them and even talk to them. He had enough spiritual insight to be aware of the elemental life-consciousness within them. Possibly he knew of the two great oaks in Glastonbury, England, Gog and Magog, which are the last two trees remaining from a sacred grove by the side of Glastonbury Tor. (This was probably part of the Processional Route used by pilgrims in the pre-Christian times up to the top of the Tor, from which you can see all over the west country of England.) Certainly this tree symbol is something which is archetypal, i.e., common to all civilizations, throughout time and place.

The Silmarillion gives the history of the world (Arda) from its creation by Eru Ilúvatar, and tells how the contradiction between the powers of Good and Evil come into being. Here Tolkien employed the same symbolism again and again. In the First Age we have the two great Lamps of the Valar, which shined throughout Arda with their radiance. When these were destroyed, they were replaced by the forces of Good with two great Trees, which radiated silver and golden light from their flowers. Each bloomed for a fixed period of time, and as the flowers of one closed, the flowers of the other opened; so for a brief period their lights shone simultaneously. Pillars are used by spiritual and mystical groups to this day, as pillars are a representation of trees. The Tree of Life of the Qabalah is composed of two pillars. According to tradition, the two pillars that stood outside Solomon's temple were hollow, and contained secret compartments known only to the High Priest, where the Torah and other artifacts could be placed in times of danger.

This symbol of the pillars reminds us that feminine and masculine energy have to work together if we are going to be successful in activating our own lives and accelerating our own evolution. Just as a tree must put down roots, so in a sense must humankind. When we do not feel "connected" with our environment—when we cease to care about finding the right place to put that scrap of litter, when we do not want to get involved when we see a criminal act being committed—we become apathetic. Once it was the business of government to make us feel as though we belonged, through education, appeals to national unity, etc. Government, when granted too much power by the people, becomes dangerous: even when the "avowed" intention of a government is to help a group of people, the end result is often greater disempowerment, greater alienation, and less personal responsibility.

Tolkien hated despotic regimes and all forms of misuse of power. Hitler was in power when Tolkien was writing *The Lord of the Rings*; Tolkien also held a strong distrust for Soviet Russia. In the domains of Morgoth, and of Sauron and Saruman, we see a land where science has gone mad; the water and the land has been poisoned by pollution, experiments are performed on captured Elves, Men, and others. In our world, we see this evil reflected in the experimentation on animals and even on humans. The use of convicted criminals, along with the offering of what, for the impoverished, is large sums of money in return for taking untested drugs is something which in our own society is obviously going to have long-term repercussions.

Tolkien was a lover of nature, and often complained about the popularity of the motor car and the expansion of the city into the countryside. The Shire is a realm where family and home are paramount, and the main objectives of life are comfort and security. By going on our own journeys, we realize the importance of these things: but while we have them around us, the faraway places and adventures seem more desirable. Rose Cotton, shown in the Empress card, seemingly occupies a very small part in the story. In fact, she is very important as an archetype: Sam thinks of her when he is exhausted on the side of Mount Doom, and these thoughts (among others) give him the strength to carry on. Tolkien must have felt similarly when he was in the trenches of World War I, being shelled and under fire, thinking of Edith waiting for him back home. The Shire is closely linked with the realm of childhood: indeed it owes much to Tolkien's own early childhood. It is possible to think of the Hobbits as children; but for each of us the Shire is a symbol of an idyllic childhood state where freedom abounds and there is no danger until the Black Riders appear.

In a sense, the journey undertaken by the Fellowship of the Ring tells us about our own journeys. By "journey" I mean one's individual life path, rather than places visited while traveling. We begin in childhood and eventually are awakened from this state by a form of initiation. Initiation rites were practiced by many tribes as a means of preparing their men and women to move from adolescence to adulthood, and to take on adult responsibilities. In our society we have very few individuals who are able to take on this initiatory role. Even though we have developed technologically as a society we are still the same as human beings. The result is that many young people create their own gangs or subculture, attendant with regalia and mores, in order to facilitate this rite of passage. Our young people need lots of outlets for their imaginations—our society does not really provide too many opportunities for expression of these energies, and sometimes even tries to suppress them. The bright child in the class is inhibited from standing out too much, in case he should make the slower kids look bad and become a target for them. Excellence should always be encouraged, and rewards given for efforts made. The Hobbits in the world today are really the children, and even the children within ourselves striving to come out.

Of the many dangers which the Companions go through, the greatest is that which they confront in the underground realm of Moria. Here Tolkien used an archetypally charged image—that of going through tunnels and dark corridors, and coming face to face with a terrible, hideous monster. This same creature is featured in Greek and other world mythologies, where the heroes (i.e., each of us) must face their worst fears and overcome them. It might be a dragon that has to be fought, or a Medusa; it might be a bull-headed creature like the Minotaur, possessing tremendous strength; or a many-headed serpent such as the Hydra. In any case, courage is the only way through. This sort of courage is hard to find. Normally it occurs only when something far greater than one's own personal safety is at stake: country, freedom, an ideal; or a person dear to one, such as one's child or partner—our concern and emotions linked to all of these give us the anger and power to overcome these monsters.

In the story of the labyrinth, in which Theseus overcomes

the Minotaur, we have a very important message: Ariadne, the king's daughter, gives Theseus a ball of string with which he is able to find his way back to the entrance of the underground realm. Without a sense of our own values, we each can become lost to our original purpose in setting out on any quest, journey, or pilgrimage. In battle, it is easy to lose sight of one's true purpose. If we lose a sense of purpose, then we have lost our ball of string, and we end up as the Minotaur, hopelessly imprisoned in our own darkness. The ancient Elven land of Lothlórien seems idyllic to us; it is a land where time stands still, where everything is beautiful and nobody has to work very hard. A vision of a land such as this which would await the faithful is common to many religions. But after a time, would we not wish to go on from there, just as our Companions did? The answer is yes, despite the comforts. This is because we need challenges and problems to overcome, and only by pitting ourselves against problems do we develop as people. People need the excitement and experience of winning, and the greater the battle, the greater the victory. Without continuous creativity, we wither and die a little bit.

The Lord of the Rings has much to teach us, if we have the eyes with which to see and the ears with which to hear. It is possible to skim though the books and miss much of their depth. The character of Gollum could be the unloved child, the one who cannot join the others because of some sort of deformity or other aspect. In his underground chamber he dwells all alone, unknown and unloved by anyone. There could be a part of his character in each of us; spend some time talking with the "unloved child" within. Gollum is, to me, the most interesting character in the story. I find the scene where he paws Frodo's sleeping body while talking to himself to be very moving. Tolkien's genius was in avoiding painting any of the characters in simplistic tones. Even the Orcs Grishnákh and Shagrat are shown with some element of character, particularly Grishnákh.

Tolkien took the name "Gandalf" and the names of the Dwarves from the Elder Edda, an ancient Icelandic text. "Gandalf" (literally "elf of the staff") means "wizard" or "magician." The image of the wizard occurs in various folklores—a man with special powers sent by the gods to help humanity against the powerful odds prevailing against it. Gandalf appears in the story, and then disappears suddenly. He turns up at a battlefield in the nick of time, or in the place where Bilbo and the Dwarves are being held prisoner, and enables their escape. Gandalf is, in a sense, a representation of God, who appears at the most unlikely times and places to help people out of the messes they have gotten themselves into. This divine presence is not ruled by pride (although Saruman tries to appeal to pride at Orthanc when he tries to win over Gandalf), but rather is full of humor, with its own quirks and eccentricities of personality. In many legends, a single person comes out of the blue and unites the warring factions under his leadership and guides the people to victory. This person always has certain powers which he is reluctant to use for personal benefit, as devotion lies in working toward the principle of good, i.e., of humanity. This image recurs in modern-day mythology: Obi-Wan Kenobi in *Star Wars* is a representation of the archetype.

The image of a savior or redeemer is deeply ingrained in the human psyche. But in our times we must reprogram what this image might mean. We must move away from understanding this image to mean that someone is going to come along and make everything fine for us. This is the illusion which every political party tries to project come election time. We must take the responsibility upon ourselves to become our own saviors and leaders, rather than neutering ourselves and giving away all our power to those who claim they will represent our interests.

I have often been asked by my students if Tolkien was a member of any magical order or esoteric study group. The answer is no. He was a Roman Catholic; his spiritual guidance came from his profound belief in Christianity and the Roman Catholic mass. He seems not to have been interested in esoterica as such. But as a Professor of English, he was steeped in the myths and traditions of the writers of the sagas and medieval poets, so some of their symbols found their way into his writing. Personally, I feel that, energy-wise, he was linked with the tradition of ancient wisdom, some of which has been carried down through the dark ages by esoteric associations such as the Rosicrucians. In any case, if we have a magical perspective, we can read through and find a great deal of magical symbolism. In the scene at Weathertop, Frodo, Aragorn, Pippin, and Merry form a circle around the fire, watching outward, awaiting the attack of the Black Riders who are looking for the Ring. This is reminiscent of the magical circles of protection cast in chalk on the floor by magicians and invokers throughout the ages.

Here we have a tip on how negative energy around us might be counteracted. Ceremonialism is something to which the human psyche is addicted. Ritual gives us symbolic control over the macrocosm. Daily rituals include washing and cleansing at the beginning or end of the day, or going to school, or exercising. Other rituals herald milestones in our lives: attaining adulthood, marriage, major anniversaries, retirement, and so forth. Ritual is important to religious practice as well: Tolkien attached great importance to, and derived great comfort from, the Roman Catholic mass. It is important to have traditions to follow in order to give ourselves a sense of continuity with the past and a link to the future. Magical practice can be thought of as a way to influence the world in which you live by making a small, easy-to-handle model of it in some representational form. The model you make might be a diagram on a piece of paper (talisman), or a set of different objects set out on an altar. Magic may or may not work objectively, but it certainly does subjectively, in the sense of getting things out of your system through a miniaturization of the forces involved in any situation. Many forward-thinking practitioners of self-healing are rediscovering that, if used properly, symbol can be a very powerful tool for redirecting consciousness and changing one's own life.

In one scene Saruman reveals his new robe to Gandalf, showing that his whiteness has been fractured into many colors. Looked at magically, this tells us to become aware of the energy fields around us. That person standing over there—does he or she emit a sense of calm, or a sense of something hidden under an outward appearance of calm? If we start really using this way of observing, we might start seeing more deeply into others, and, as always, ourselves. Some may say that to see in this way would come as a shock; it surely would, but it is better to be aware than not, especially given the chances of enhancing your own survival by doing so. We have all made mistakes in our lives, and we can learn from these mistakes. But if we had known what problems would result from a particular course of action, how much suffering might we have avoided? If we could "see" when a drunken motorist might suddenly swerve into our path;

see when and where a terrorist group was going to strike; see where a train was going to jump its rails—how much suffering would we avoid, if not for ourselves, then for others?

This is one reason for developing our psychic potential—so that we might become a more effective friend of humans and help others in their life's journeys. Training concentration to function this way is one of the challenges confronting the human race at this point. For the story of *The Lord of the Rings* is not only our own individual story; it is the story of our entire race on this planet and its history. The unfolding of powers within us can be attained by spiritual development, for without the necessary spiritual qualities, the acquisition of powers will just turn us into Saruman-like figures, and we add to our karmic debt. Without knowledge of the implications of what we do, we are likely to create more misery than we clear up. Recall the scene where Gandalf refuses to touch the Ring when Frodo offers it to him. Gandalf says that in seeking to become wise, he would become as terrible as the Dark Lord himself—and with about as much negative karma to carry!

One of the most satisfying aspects of *The Lord of the Rings*, for me, is that the decent people win in the end. Victory comes not through the strength of their arms, their weaponry, or their magical powers: triumph over the evil forces is the result of loyalty and a shared mission to take the Ring to Mount Doom. Ethics—following one's belief as to what is right or wrong—is the greatest force that there is. Deep within, we all know the right course of action to take in any situation. Sometimes things happen quickly and we may well make a mistake. But if, instead of reacting to provocation out of immediate impulse, we were to find a quiet space and think things through, we might arrive at better solutions. Frodo goes off to think by himself just before the Company is parted. In a scene rather like the garden of Gethsemene, he is deep in solitary contemplation, wondering what he is going to have to do. Each time Frodo offers the Ring to someone he feels is more qualified to deal with the situation, like Gandalf or Galadriel, he is refused. Remember that Moses argued with God and tried to get away from his own destiny; similarly, Frodo is that part of each of us which feels vulnerable and weak in the face of life's battles.

J. R. R. Tolkien's father died when Tolkien was four years old, his mother when he was twelve. In order to understand Tolkien's world, these facts must be given some consideration. Mabel Tolkien's conversion to Catholicism had alienated her strongly Protestant family. So after her death, the Tolkien boys lived in various boarding houses. At sixteen, Tolkien fell in love with Edith Bratt. But his ward, Father Morgan, kept the two apart until Tolkien turned twenty-one. Although Tolkien remained faithful and loyal throughout his marriage to Edith, he never truly knew women and cast them as distant goddess-like figures in his works.

The role of women in *The Lord of the Rings* has been criticized, as women are largely kept out of the main action and relegated to secondary roles. The main exception is Lady Éowyn's defeat of the Nazgûl Captain. The Lady Arwen is not involved in any battles, nor is the Lady Galadriel. But the battles, which men consider to be the central areas of attention, are not necessarily the most important aspects of the story. The battle for Minas Tirith was not central to the outcome. What was central was the scene on the side of Mount Doom, in which Frodo finds that he cannot throw the Ring into the fiery furnace. Yet the women in

The Lord of the Rings, in their roles as sources of inspiration, become far greater through what they symbolize than in what they say or do. The love he bears for Lady Arwen pushes Aragorn to fulfill his quest; he must fulfill his destiny if he is to take her hand in marriage.

The Lady Galadriel functions as the giver of visions and important gifts to the Company when they leave Lothlórien. Galadriel gives Frodo the Phial of light which saves him and the entire quest when he is captured in Shelob's lair. Galadriel is the goddess, the healer, the diviner of the future; beautiful, enchanting, wise. I believe that Galadriel comes closer to Tolkien's deepest awareness of women; she represents his mother, his creator, the beautiful, brave, independent, and learned woman who had forsaken all for her faith, the woman he could never know. For Tolkien, the role of women was more inspirational than actual, whereas in much of recent fantasy writing, women are often shown in a sword-bearing capacity.

In the formation of the Fellowship of the Ring at the Council of Elrond, the "team members" or Companions are selected by Elrond to go on the quest to return the Ring to its source of creation. He chooses from each of the races of the Free Peoples: Dwarves, Elves, Men, and Hobbits. They leave Rivendell with a pony. They are assisted at various times by the great Eagles. Together, they represent the world of nature with all of its different tribes, races, breeds, and forms of expression ultimately united in the face of the common enemy. We can see this reflected in the world around us, where the real dangers have become nuclear waste, pollution, the leveling of the great rain forests, loss of species, runaway population growth. All beings must come together as one tribe in order to solve these challenges to our survival. There was great distrust between Dwarves and Elves, yet Gimli the Dwarf and Legolas the Elf overcame the differences of the past; so humankind will be put to the test to overcome our present status quo in order to embrace a new era.

Saruman tells Gandalf that a new era is about to open on Middle-earth, one that forces people to work either with it or against it. From the way Saruman speaks, we know that he has been shown a "vision" of the "inevitability" of Mordor's victory. Perhaps Tolkien believed this in moments of depression; he must have felt something of this around him. England was in the midst of World War II and would soon lose its Empire; the ordered way of life was being replaced by a very different society. But, in a sense deeper than Tolkien perhaps realized at the time of writing, a new era was opening up for the world, scientifically and economically.

Never before have different cultures and countries been so closely tied to one another as now. With the Internet, satellite television, new telecommunication systems, and new sources of power, what occurs in one place now more than ever has an impact or effect around the rest of the world. Chernobyl brought this home to a lot of people. Up until that time, there had never really been the awareness that a nuclear fallout in one person's backyard could affect the washing on the line at home. This new era is opening up, not just collectively, but for each of us as individuals. This means that we are going to be faced with the challenges of both adapting to this new world and of leading it, and of directing the evolutionary processes as we do so. For each of us, this process is going to require putting aside certain notions of how things work in order to gain a new perspective. It will require adaptability, flexibility, and a certain mental and spiritual dexterity.

Aragorn is a warrior archetype, the negative and destructive aspects of which we can see in the violence and war in our world. The higher qualities of the warrior are seen in defending the weak, the defenseless, those who have few rights and less power. The warrior archetype in its positive aspect is sorely needed in our world—though not necessarily for fighting with swords! One can fight with the mighty pen. Pens deliver messages of anger and dissatisfaction to governments, and allow people to communicate monumental ideas with many others near and far. We must also be prepared to exercise courage as warriors in our own lives when faced with battles that seem much bigger than we can handle.

Aragorn is the part of each of us which is noble and royal (in the true sense of the term). He appears in the story as a Ranger. Rangers were men living out in the wilderness, keeping the supply lines open, and keeping an eye on what was going on in distant regions. They would each have to fend for themselves for the long periods when they were far away from any town or village. They are similar to the pioneers who opened up America, taking their families and possessions with them as they set off into the great unknown. In our society the qualities of freedom and independence that so strongly motivated these pioneers are still prized, although not necessarily in the same way; each of us might feel less brave when we compare ourselves with their heroism. But we face a different kind of adventure: a journey into our own inner space. A new expression of bravery will formulate itself as humanity grows and develops. I personally believe our course of evolution will involve the unfolding of such psychic abilities as telepathy and astral projection.

The Orcs are rather like the demons or deposed gods of any mythology—those that have been cast down from a better state to inhabit a hell-like place. The Orcs are the unintelligent underlings who do the bidding of their evil master without too much thinking. They are aggressive, even amongst each other, and destructive of anything which has beauty, even when the destruction serves no purpose to them.

The Orcs are with us in every society. They are the hooligans, the criminals. They are those in the world who have been brain-washed, conditioned to believe everything their "masters" tell them; the fanatics who for the sake of religion or politics will plant a bomb or shoot somebody in the back. They are not the real cause of the world's problems. Many of the world's problems are deliberately caused by people who stand to gain money or power from artificially-generated problems.

The Orc type often tries to get something without working for it, and, if acquisition is impossible, they will sabotage it instead. There is no reasoning with this breed. Only force will get through to the Orcs; and in Middle-earth as in our world today force must be used to keep them at bay. In order to protect good, those that do evil must be recognized and discouraged.

The Elves can be thought of as the artists and musicians, those who are involved in cultural pursuits or intellectual pursuits of any nature. Elves, renowned for their sophistication and craftsmanship, advance and maintain knowledge and achievement, pushing back the boundaries of knowledge with their discoveries. The Dwarves may symbolize those that labor diligently; they constantly dig into the ground in their never-ending search for the precious silvery metal Mithril and other ores. To be successful in our world, we must each embody elements of both Elves and Dwarves. It is not enough to be hard-working; to be totally Dwarvish would make one difficult to get to know. A Dwarf-type would only issue commands and would constantly function in work-mode. Of course, not all elements of the Dwarf character are negative; with hard work we arrive at our destinations, and persistence is important in many aspects of life—but only up to a point. After a certain point, any positive can become a negative. Those who fall under the spell of the Dwarves become workaholics, burying their problems in piles of work. When their work-lives are over, they do not know what to do, and very often they die (either emotionally or physically) after a year or so in retirement. The Elvish qualities of inspiration, intelligence, ingenuity, and sheer style can work wonders for us: finding new solutions to old problems, charming even the fiercest opponent into approachability or submission. We could all learn much from the Elves in terms of finding new ways to communicate with others. But we must not become too Elvish either: turning our backs on the world in our search for beauty, or substituting talk for action.

Encounters between humans and other races have often been depicted in literature as being problematic. There is the ubiquitous legend of the man who loves the fairy maiden or the mermaid who, after marrying him and even bearing his children, deserts him and goes back to her own race, leaving the man desolate and bereft. The female in these stories represents the soul of the man which he finds and tries to hold onto for a while, and in so doing actually loses. Perhaps this is what is represented by the myriad races in *The Lord of the Rings*—something of the soul of humanity is within them, waiting for us to find it.

The weapons in *The Lord of the Rings* are quite revealing. The swords that the Companions of the Fellowship use have names and, we suspect, personalities. Swords represent dedication, and the broken sword Aragorn carries reminds us that he must reforge the kingdom after it has been broken apart. For this to happen, the hero must be prepared to undergo transformation—usually death, a wound, or a sacrifice. Only through such a transformation can the kingdom clean out its old wounds and begin to heal. In ancient times, the people would slay the king if the land became infertile, for they thought that the king's life force had become sluggish. Aragorn is the 39th descendent of Isildur, who cut off Sauron's finger and claimed the Ring after Sauron had been overcome in battle by Isildur's father King Elendil. Aragorn's purpose is to fulfill the work of his ancestors in overcoming the influence of Sauron again. Yet he is not ruthless. He shows skill in strategy and tactics, and exercises bravery when it is necessary, but is never rash. As one who has experienced privations for a long period, he can live off the land and shows freedom from the limitations of life. Aragorn is crowned King of Gondor and Arnor at the end of the story, rather than Faramir, brother of Boromir. Aragorn also represents the principle of choice and selectivity. He demonstrates great self-control when he renounces the love of Lady Éowyn, and illustrates the idealistic (i.e., higher) functions of human love, which are almost a spiritual experience.

The Rings themselves are the most important magical

objects in *The Lord of the Rings*. There were, all in all, twenty of them. The Three were forged by the Elves, but without Sauron's assistance, which is why they were less affected by his influence. They each had a red, white, or blue stone. The red ruby set in gold, in the possession of Gandalf, represents the element of fire, and Gandalf is the "servant of the Secret Fire" as he reveals in his confrontation with the Balrog. This Ring represents the qualities of action, courage, and initiative. The blue stone was actually a sapphire, also set in gold. Owned by Elrond, it was the Ring of the element of air, symbol of the power of the mind, thought, and reason. The white Ring was owned by Galadriel, and its stone was securely set in delicate Mithril. It was the Ring of Water, representing feelings, emotions, and intuition. Thus the Three represent three of the four elements. The missing element is earth: and it is mastery over the material universe that the One Ring actually confers. Earth is the element through which the other three express their influences—it is the most immovable of the elements, yet this is precisely the quality which gives it its durability. It is the means through which all energy finally manifests.

After these Rings, there are Nine for Mortal Men, and Seven for the Dwarves. These Rings were made by Sauron and the Elves together, and Sauron captured them and distributed them throughout Middle-earth some short time later. When the Dwarves put on their Rings, Sauron was furious to find himself unable to control them, for Dwarves do not submit to the will of others. The Rings made for Mortal Men were, however, much more effective, and it was over the human race that Sauron's influence came to be mostly felt. The One Ring was made last of all, when Sauron forged it in the fires of Mount

Doom and programmed it with his personal force. The Ruling Ring was made of plain gold without any stone, and bore no distinctive markings. Only when it was heated in the fire would it show the thin letters in the language of the Black Speech of Mordor, but written in fine Elven lettering:

"One Ring to rule them all, One Ring to find them,
One Ring to bring them all and in the darkness bind them."

III
The Major Arcana

In the tarot, the Major Arcana represents the 22 mysteries of life's journey. At one time or another in each of our lives, we go through the experiences represented on each of the cards, both Major and Minor. The Minor Arcana represents 56 everyday life situations and people that we have known, or will come across in the future.

The Major Arcana represents the major themes of learning that we all go through. They show us explanations, as it were, as to how each of us may live more fulfilling and effective lives by applying the lessons of each card. In approaching the Major Arcana, we will derive different meaning and significance at different points in our lives. What any one card may have to offer us at one point in life may well differ at a later point. As we go through life, just as our lessons change, so the meaning or message which each card carries changes over time. Contained within each card are themes from mythological tales, folklore, Biblical stories, and legends from around the world.

A note regarding artistic interpretation in The Lord of the Rings Tarot deck. Throughout the scenes presented in the deck, the Hobbits are depicted as wearing shoes. It states quite clearly in *The Hobbit* that "Hobbits seldom wore shoes." We have taken the word "seldom" literally—meaning "not never." In fact, there were many different groups of Hobbits—the Hobbits from Eastfarthing, for example, "wore Dwarf-boots in muddy weather." While Hobbits have generally been drawn without shoes in most of the artistic representations throughout the 1970s and 1980s; we feel that for our own representation, if one considers the great journeys which these Hobbits underwent far beyond the borders of their small Shire, it would be a trivialization of the Hobbits not to be shown wearing shoes or boots. Also, some scenes depicted on the cards are composite scenes or symbolic representations to portray a particular tarot meaning. These representations are noted in the descriptions of the cards.

0 THE FOOL

Gollum sits by the side of a waterfall, having just caught a fish. He is pondering whether or not to eat it, or just throw it back into the water. The One Ring is at one side of the pond, hidden under a clump of grass. Above Gollum shines the full moon—"white face," he calls it. Gollum never liked the moon—or the sun ("yellow face"), for that matter. Both, he believed, would betray him. The moon represents the subconscious, while the sun represents the conscious mind. For Gollum, both aspects of awareness are unpleasant, and are to be avoided.

Gollum belongs ultimately on neither "side," neither that of good nor that of bad. He is a creature who has chosen to dwell in the darkness, but is not aligned with the organized evil of Mordor. He is a chaotic element in the War of the Ring, motivated by an overwhelming yearning for the One Ring, and yet implacably opposed to seeing it returned to either Sauron or the fires of Mount Doom. When Gollum realizes that Frodo is actually attempting to destroy the Ring, he attempts to save "the Precious," and in biting off Frodo's finger he falls back into the fires, taking the Ring with him. In fact, Frodo would not have had the strength to have renounced the Ring, so great had its influence on him become. Gollum's intervention allowed the Ring to be destroyed.

Gandalf, right from the beginning, felt that Gollum's role was going to be a significant one. Gollum hated both sunlight and moonlight. Here he is shown squinting by night. The Ring on the right is depicted as showing the Elven script, which would actually only be visible after being heated in fire.

Gollum also represents guilt and consequential withdrawal from the world. When we act in a negative manner, or commit sins of omission, we then tend to withdraw from those against whom we have committed those actions and live life in isolation and alienation. Taking responsibility for one's actions remedies this situation. Gollum began by stealing from his neighbors, and thereby effectively excluded himself from being a member of the community. An individual who continues to operate in this way goes on a dwindling spiral and eventually withdraws from society into psychosis.

TAROT MEANING

An influence, event, or meeting with someone in which the unexpected happens, completely changing the course of your life. A new chapter of life's experience is opening up, and it is necessary to put away all of the emotional baggage which has accumulated over time. The fool heralds the discovery of an idea, an invention, a flash of inspiration which changes one's course of action.

Consider your own experiences. Who are the fools: those who live by the judgments of others—or those who give up trying to meet the expectations of others, and instead live up to their own potential?

In medieval times, it was the job of the fool, the court jester, to take the tension out of certain situations; it is through humor and play that this archetype teaches us the most. It is a very exciting energy to work with, and one which needs a certain ability to channel, as it can get out of hand once you have contacted it. Those that get swept away by this archetype often end up losing everything out of irresponsibility. All of the gods are within us, but each one needs to be brought out and given full expression. We cannot allow any one archetype to dominate us completely. But sometimes we each need the energy to break the spell of seriousness. In my experience teaching tarot, I come across many people who think they need a lot of schooling to learn how to read the cards; they are often surprised how easy it is to learn once they connect with this energy.

ASTROLOGICAL ASSOCIATION

The planet Uranus, planet of eccentricity and rebellion.

Uranus spins from its top vertically, unlike all the other planets in the solar system, which spin around their "bellies." Similarly, Gollum has his own agenda, his own individual sense of right and wrong, and is not a part of any side. All he wants is to find the Ring again and own it, while hiding under the mountain from where he was able to avoid the searching gaze of Sauron. He used the Ring not for commanding great armies, nor for magical feats, but for catching food and sneaking around to avoid the goblins.

We all have some element of Gollum within us, for he represents our own rebelliousness, and our refusal to live our lives in accordance with other people's dictates or expectations. He also represents our own inability to see the potential within something, even if that something is ourselves. Gollum could not conceive of using the Ring for anything else. He could, theoretically, have become more ambitious, but he didn't. He was unconcerned with these aspects of life, preferring his own company in the darkness.

Gollum's story is that of the unindividuated soul, being thrust out by fate into the outer world (his leaving the mountain lake is symbolic of a kind of birth). His journey is that of a soul trying to find its identity, its mission, regardless of the price which must be paid for by the lives of others, or even its own.

THE FOOL SPEAKS

Yes, my preciousesss, I know it'sss here somewhere. Can feel it, close by. More haste, less speed. These nice bony fishesssess fill my belly, but can they stop the aching void in my soul since I lost the Precious? No, I don't think so…I would so like to find the Preciousss again, my love, where are you, my love?

I am Gollum, the unloved child. I am alone in my underworld hell. I show the influence of obsession, of extreme desires which need to be released, and from which I need to transcend. I represent all that you never took responsibility for, which has come back to visit you. My road is just beginning, and stretches out ahead of me into the future. Sometimes when I look into my future I see myself as very different from how I now am—as how

I might yet become. I am my own equal and opposite: I am honest, yet not; trustworthy, yet not.

I come in the dark to teach you the relevance of that which you would prefer not to confront. Confrontation doesn't have to mean a battle: it means being able to look long and deeply at something without flinching. When we confront a fear or a problem, it vanishes. If we approach a matter in the spirit of truth, the answers are nearly always plainly revealed. The great truths which we claim to seek are usually to be found in that which we cannot easily confront. As Jesus said, "And you will know the truth, and the truth will make you free." (John 8:32)

I THE MAGICIAN

Gandalf stands facing you. All around him are various symbols connected with his work. In his left hand he holds his staff: we have depicted him with a crystal ball at the top which emanates flames. Gandalf is a servant of the Secret Fire, the fire of God that illumines the souls of humanity.

On his lapel he wears the upward-pointing triangle linking him with this element, while above him shines the Elven Ring Narya—the Red Ring, set with a ruby—one of the Three hidden in Middle-earth from Sauron, who desired them for the greater power they would give him. On his forehead is the runic "G," the initial of his name. Gandalf was the second greatest of the Istari (wizards) who were incarnated and sent to Middle-earth to counterbalance the power of the Dark Lord in favor of humanity.

Gandalf was known as Gandalf the Grey, or Mithrandir, the Grey Pilgrim (as he was affectionately termed), due to his devotional quality and sense of compassion toward the little people, the common-folk, and the animals. He was accepting of all, fierce and unyielding in his opposition to evil, and totally devoted to his duty of helping humanity at every step. On the stone upon which he stands we see inscribed a labyrinth. It could be a map, perhaps showing the way through the Mines of Moria, his (and our!) journey through the Underworld. Here we must face our greatest fear (symbolized by the Balrog), and sacrifice our lower selves, so that our inner essence can escape back to the higher realms of light and freedom. It is also a symbol of the element earth itself, showing that all of our actions must be grounded in reality. Unless we stand firmly in our lives honoring our commitments and duties, how can we aspire to the spiritual and magical heights to which Gandalf promises to lead us?

In his right hand he holds the great sword Glamdring, whose name means "foe-hammer," and which here symbolizes the element air. On the hilt of our sword is a bird's head, representing the heights to which our thoughts may soar, and our need to retain our sense of vision lest we lose our way and become overwhelmed with the mundane aspects of our reality. The sword is a symbol of battle, but here the delicate poising on its tip suggests that nowadays it should be used not to "destroy the enemy," but rather to look for the causes of problems. It is all too easy to "pick up the sword" and start attacking others, blaming them for whatever displeases us. The sword here is shown as a kind of scalpel, to be used for gently prying out negativity at its root, to allow more positive influences to function. The sword is therefore not a symbol of brutal power imposing a single will upon a subjugate people, but of the use of reason in order to resolve differences.

At Gandalf's feet we see a beautiful golden chalice. It is tipped slightly to one side, as if inviting us to drink from it. It represents the emotional aspect of life, and signifies that there is much more love and friendship around us than we imagine. In fact, the entire story of *The Lord of the Rings* is about how friendship, love, and loyalty among friends overcomes all the negativity of the world. This tipped chalice invites us to experience the great abundance of love and friendship lying around us. It is a gift offered to us—there is no price for it.

Gandalf is a symbol of the inner teacher—that inner voice of wisdom and enlightenment which comes to us from above, if we can still the mind's noise long enough to be able to hear it.

One of Gandalf's great qualities is his sense of fun, and his ability to amuse and inspire ordinary folk. He represents the many "magicians" in our midst: those people who in their own small way are working toward a better tomorrow for humanity, unselfish in their devotion, not needing the praises of others in order to continue with what they are doing. Gandalf is shown without his hat on—he didn't always wear it!

TAROT MEANING

The use of reason, discussion, debate, and thought in order to create change. Resolving problems at their foundation. Gandalf's intention was to defeat Sauron by eliminating the Ring itself, not by opposing him with armies. Gandalf did wield a sword when necessary, although he knew an important battle of a different kind was to take place involving Frodo on Mount Doom.

This card also represents putting across our messages in a way that will convince other people of the validity of our ideas. Gandalf repeatedly had to use all his powers of persuasion to awaken people to the danger they were in: both King Théoden and Denethor the Steward of Gondor, leaders of their people, had come under the influence of Darkness (Théoden under Saruman through Wormtongue, Denethor under Sauron through the Palantír).

A magician is anyone who acts as an intermediary between the world of "above" and the physical world of "below," rather like a stylus on a record which will pick up the "messages" on the record grooves and translate the indentations into sound. Gandalf came as one of the team of five wizards led by Saruman, who later betrayed his original mission. Gandalf represents that aspect of ourselves which has a mission and follows it through. Everyone has a mission in life, and each is as significant as Gandalf's—that is, to grow and develop spiritually so that we can each act as a better channel through which the higher cosmic forces can flow down to this earthly plane and manifest.

The negative aspect of the magician is Saruman, whose abilities are misused for destructive or selfish ends. Saruman can be considered to be the "shadow self." He is portrayed in a destructive mode, but within ourselves it is more helpful to think of our shadow selves as being composed of those experiences in which we have lost or compromised our principles. It would be easy to bring fear into the exploration of our unknown selves, but let us consciously relax and approach ourselves more in wonder than rejection.

Negative manifestations of this card in our world include the Saruman-like attributes of smooth talking (his voice) and illusion (his robe of many colors). We are constantly bombarded with illusory images on television and film; do these images reflect society's values or influence them? The human mind is susceptible to images cast before it, as almost anything can be made to seem desirable, heroic, or sexy. We need to be aware of the influence such media has on children; it is staggering to realize that the average youngster actually witnesses up to 8,000 killings on television by the end of elementary school! Unfortunately, the price of free speech and independence of the press is the occasional misuse of power through providing negative illusions.

ASTROLOGICAL ASSOCIATION

The planet Mercury, symbol of communication, especially across great distances.

The Romans would make sacrifices at Mercury's shrines before traveling to the more distant parts of the Empire, and invoked his blessing on all matters concerning commerce and trade. He was a clever god, and could persuade anyone to do virtually anything.

Mercury was also known as Hermes in the Greek mythology and Thoth Tehuti in the Egyptian. In fact, versions of Mercury have appeared in the mythology of every society since the dawn of humanity to educate human beings—he teaches letters and numbers, trigonometry and mathematics, architecture, and medicine. He is the symbol of intellectual power, and how the applied use of logic and reason can be used to rid the world of many of its evils, like disease, ignorance, and illiteracy.

In Aztec mythology he appears as the blond-haired, blue-eyed Quetzalcoatl, who leads his people away from the practice of human sacrifice and enables them to build a better civilization.

Under his guidance, they learn agriculture and become able to organize themselves into cities in a humane society. Eventually Quetzalcoatl builds a ship to return to his homeland far to the east, beyond the rising sun. (A parallel scene occurs at the Grey Havens when Gandalf and the Ringbearers leave Middle-earth to sail west beyond the Great Sea to the Undying Lands.) When Quetzalcoatl departs, the people resort to their barbarous ways and the human sacrifices are resumed.

In the Norse tradition, he appears in a negative aspect as Loki, who uses his cunning to establish his will against other deities, and is the epitome of trickery. In our lives, the negative Magician is the salesman or trickster who gets us to sign a document before we've even had a chance to read it through. We are furious with ourselves afterwards, needless to say, but what can we do then? Some professional negative magicians are the con-men, who go from one person to another tricking them out of their life savings and then disappearing. Their lies are so convincing, you can't catch them out.

Other elements of the Magician card relate to advertising, which works on such a clever level as to actually bypass the reasoning faculty, and induces in people a desire to own something which defies all reason (only by owning a particular product can you really begin to feel complete—masculine, feminine, wise, a good family man, etc.). We find the same thing with those who set up religious cults that snare the lonely, the unwary, and the vulnerable into their webs with suggestions that life will get better or more meaningful for them once they join and dedicate their worldly goods to the good of the group.

Well, here you are. It took you a long time to find me. I've been waiting for you to catch up with me for some time now. Anyway, you're here now. Sit down a moment. Have a drink from my chalice—there, that's better. Refreshing, isn't it? You'll feel like a new you in a moment or so.

I have a gift for you. Here, feel the stone of my ring as I press it against your forehead. Do you feel it getting warmer there? Good. Let the warmth run down the length of your spine, right to its base. My, my, you are warming up now, aren't you?

Let the warmth stay there for a minute or two. Let the heat move across through your body now. You are coming more alive, I can see. What a receptive student you are turning into! If only all of my initiates were as clear as you!

Now, I want you to let that warmth start to run upwards along your spine, slowly does it. Let it move across the spot on the other side of your belly button, now up further, further, parallel to your heart, very good. Let it trickle right up through the nape of your neck, into your head, up, up, up, till it warms up the top-most part of your head. Now, do things seem a little different than they did before? Good, and so they should! So they should!

I want you to practice this exercise often; not at any fixed time, particularly, but just as a state of awareness which you can slide into while on the bus or train, or even walking along. Incorporate it into your everyday life. You don't need to tell anyone what you are doing—they probably wouldn't understand anyway. That's why magic has been kept secret for all these years; because people fear that which they cannot understand.

Welcome to my order—you are now an Initiate of the Order of the Secret Fire. By developing the Secret Fire within yourself, you will strengthen yourself for all the challenges and ordeals which lie ahead. Look at the forces and temptations I was up against! Well, you will be able to do the same, and come out on top, if you practice this faithfully.

I will be off now, but I will be looking in on you to make sure that you are practicing this technique. Bet you never thought that self-empowerment could be passed on so directly! Don't give up on your books, but get working on that technique: you'll only understand why it is so important when you actually do it!

II THE HIGH PRIESTESS

The High Priestess is draped in a robe of purple, which represents high rank, especially of a spiritual nature. This is the Lady Éowyn, of the Royal House of Rohan. In her hand she holds a scroll, which represents her orders from her uncle King Théoden to stay behind and guard the women and children. This she finds totally impossible to do. She knows that destiny has summoned her to play a more active part in the ensuing battle between Light and Darkness than to remain in the background where nothing much will happen. She holds the scroll tightly, about to tear it up and throw it to the ground. Already she has donned her fighting armor, for she will fight as well and as bravely as any male warrior of either Gondor or Rohan. She does not yet know it, but soon she will fight the Witch-king, the Ringwraiths' Captain, behead his Nazgûl steed, and slay him.

Éowyn stands between two main sets of pillars: one is light, and the other set is a porchway or entrance in black, signifying that the quality she represents is the very doorway between yin and yang, namely active and passive, giving and receiving. She is guardian to the temple which we see behind her, albeit in a state of ruin. She is the link between our heritage and today; without her, we would be little better than Orcs, a people with no history, traditions, culture, or value.

In her hand Éowyn holds her sword, which signifies her determination, and her calling to her duty—not the will of others so much as her own awareness of her real calling in life. She deeply loved Aragorn, and wanted to become his wife and lifelong companion. Although he rebuffed her several times, in the end none too subtly, in her heart Éowyn knew that Aragorn was not intended for her. She had great intuition, an ability to feel what was going on below the surface of visible reality (misleading, at times), and to let her own inner voice be her guide to action. That she disobeyed orders worked out for the best, as no man alive could slay the Witch-king. But she remained committed to her own truth, and that is the lesson she has for each of us.

Above her shines the crescent moon, representing the flux of all situations, the malleability of the material universe, and how things transmute over time. It also reminds us to have patience; if things don't work out as we would like, let us have a bit more patience until the conditions turn around again and the tide comes in. Then we can act with a certainty of victory!

On her side we see a shield, and the White Horse of Rohan upon it is depicted as the Uffington horse of Wiltshire plain—an ancient Celtic site, although sacred to Celts and Saxons alike, and used by both on their shields and banners. The arch behind her is black, thus referring to the darker side of the High Priestess in her role as Queen of the Night.

The High Priestess is one of the more difficult cards for many people to understand. Some believe that in ancient times, people were almost universally ruled by women, as women were capable of bringing new human beings into the world through the magical experience of childbirth. Women were fierce warriors in those days, easily equal to men in battle and the hunt.

In all mythologies we find the ever-recurring theme of a battle between a male hero—Zeus, Hercules, Marduk, Fafnir, St. George, to mention but a few—and a dragon. This type of battle can be read as a symbol of the fight between the previous matriarchal cultures and the advent of the patriarchal system through the rise of the Aryans and the creation of their civilization. Through their mastery of the element fire, and the subsequent smelting of metals for use in weapons for hunting and fighting, they were able to subjugate other cultures that were less advanced technologically, but more in tune with nature, the seasons, and the elements. This same pattern can be found in other world cultures as well, including China. The defeat of the dragon could be interpreted as the defeat of the power of women, and their subsequent enslavement by men as chattels in a state of slavery and ignorance. So fearful have the ruling patriarchs been of women's power that whenever women have even been suspected of posing a threat to their governance, they have instigated various forms of persecutions or witch-hunts.

The High Priestess ruled over all the other priestesses, presiding at their ceremonies and acting as the physical counterpart of the goddess, from whom all life, health, and well-being flowed. Thus she was the goddess whose blessings were sought out through the ancient ceremonies, fertility rites, and acts of magical association with the forces of nature. More recently, there has been a great revival of interest in the spiritual tradition of which the High Priestess is/was the symbol, with many people exploring paganism, druidry, etc.

As a symbol of the feminine and the unconscious, the High Priestess represents the subconscious processes at work: our survival instinct that kept our ancestors alive in the times of ferocious wild beasts and incredibly adverse circumstances. This instinct would "tell" them when to move south, which clump of innocent-looking trees to avoid, and when to run away as quickly as their legs could carry them, even though they might not be able to see any danger, and their slowly developing conscious minds would be unable to see why. When this instinct becomes blunted, we become infinitely more vulnerable to danger.

Because of her association with the "hidden parts of the mind," the High Priestess also represents the issues deep in our minds that we encounter when we set out on our journey toward greater self-realization. In this journey we become aware of our feelings. For instance, how do you feel right this minute? Or when you see so and so? This journey will involve allowing ourselves to feel all these emotions without being judgmental, because we tend to monitor our own feelings and censor them. Before we can pass through the doorway of the subconscious realm into the dimension of superconsciousness, we must resolve inner personality conflicts to the point where we can function, if not necessarily become "perfect people." We will always "have issues"—but we must work on clarifying our subconscious realm, at least to the point where we are not reacting/overreacting to life situations in a manner that defies all reason.

In a person's spread, this card can sometimes show the relevance of therapy or counseling, as today the High Priestess is someone who is able to guide you to looking at your own patterns in life, thereby enabling you to begin to transcend them.

Another aspect of this card is silence, for the High Priestess does not speak, but experiences and feels. Whereas the Magician embodied principles of activation and energy, here the condition is inert and latent. The High Priestess tends toward waiting rather than acting; postponement rather than fulfillment. It could be argued that the Lady Galadriel could as well occupy this placement, with her visionary mirror (the moon) and her kingdom where time stands still. But Tolkien lived in a class-ridden and misogynistic English society which did not encourage women or people from "the lower orders" to come forward. And people higher on the social scale also had it ingrained that they should not be too aggressive or extroverted. There was a great amount of energy spent on inhibition and self-limitation!

ASTROLOGICAL ASSOCIATION
The moon, symbol of the mother.

The moon brings in the tide, and draws it away again. How amazing that such an apparently small disk shining in the night sky so far away can have such a powerful influence on planet earth! It also affects plants, herbs, and people's minds. It brings things into being, and diminishes them again. It is the symbol of growth (new moon), fulfillment (full moon), and decline (waning phase). Thus the moon shows us how our lives must inevitably develop, over time, and all things which we go through and experience as part of our lives. Éowyn, after the War of the Ring, married Faramir of Gondor, and became a "Mother for her people."

The moon also represents the subconscious realm, which contains all the memories of our ancestors and is the doorway into the realm of superconscious experience. Modern man has become too engrossed with his fascination of the Magician's technological wonders (gimmicks). He has lost touch with his deepest feelings and emotions. In order to shield himself from the intensity of these feelings, he will make jokes about them, but deep down he fears what they may show him.

The moon apparently moves through the entire zodiac (all twelve signs) in less than the course of a calendar month (about 23 days). It is thus the fastest-moving heavenly body in the cosmic sky, and is held astrologically to be the "trigger" for the most immediate changes which occur in our lives. It brings into being those things which sit on the edge of the astral plane half in, half out of our physical reality. It nudges them into being, giving them a chance to "become" something. If they do not succeed, then they too will diminish and begin to decay back into a primal state of non-existence.

THE HIGH PRIESTESS SPEAKS

I am the High Priestess, and none come into the realms of anything higher than mundane awareness except through me. Behind me you see the doorway which leads into the inner sanctum of the symbolic Temple of Initiation. Your friend the Magician has already given you an initiation of sorts. That is well and good, but let me remind you, in your state of youthful arrogance, that there are many other powers at work in this universe other than his alone. To pass between the two pillars there has to be some test of your worthiness. In tribal societies, before a boy could be considered a man, he would have to pass some test of courage, such as spending a certain number of days alone in a forest, or a period of time underground.

I am the priestess from the days of tribalism, before the colonizing of alien patriarchal powers—Romans, Greeks, Egyptian, Parthians, whoever—came and established themselves in your lands. In those days you were all ruled by women, who would lead your men into battle. Even ancient historians have written about my Celtic sisters and the terror they struck into the hearts of the Roman soldiers when they attempted to conquer their lands. In those days you were closer to nature, to your tribal side, and you realized the value of staying with your own people. In those days any fraternization with outsiders was dangerous, and could lead to your being captured and enslaved.

You may remember—if some of your past lives were based around those times—that quite a bit of religious worship was based around the moon and its phases, with sacrifices and orgies at specific times when the heavenly bodies had grouped themselves around the earth in certain patterns.

Don't forget that although those times have changed, I am still very much with you. Deny me at your own risk. Block yourself against my voice and you will likely end up in a therapist's chair—or worse. Those of you who think you are being "cosmic" or "spiritual" without having met me first are deluding yourselves: in reality, you are nothing but pie-in-the-sky types, looking for signs and wonders but unaware of the great mysteries which lie hidden within yourselves.

III The Empress

In the center is Galadriel; on the left Bilbo (as a baby) is held by his mother, Belladonna Took; and on the right is Rose Cotton, who eventually married Sam Gamgee and gave him thirteen children. Thirteen is the ancient pagan number of completion, there being thirteen months within a solar return or year; thus thirteen completed the one as a holy number, and pertained also to the feminine mysteries. It is possible that Tolkien was unaware of this, but unconsciously "painted" into the story a symbol which brings the history of Middle-earth into completion: the cosmic or royal marriage, in which masculine and feminine aspects cease fighting and learn to cooperate with each other and help each other achieve their mutual objectives and balance their respective qualities (feminine/passivity, emotion; masculine/action, materialism).

Galadriel represents that part of our souls which is beautiful, and is seen as such by those around us. When our inner beauty shines through, it illuminates the entire body. Galadriel also represents romanticism—in the original love story of Tristan and Isolde, the enchanting woman represents the soul of the man who seeks her.

When offered the Ring, Galadriel was able to disassociate herself from the Ring's direct influence, but it made an appeal to her need for beauty and recognition. The empress brings a great deal of beauty into her everyday life. The dissolution of barriers is often her greatest difficulty, as is giving too much of herself without allowing the other person to reciprocate.

The empress in her earthly capacity brings into being many different kinds of life. She will, in her capacity as goddess of nature, try to sustain those she can, but if the environment begins to get killed off by greedy and overzealous hunters/croppers unconcerned with maintaining the vital ecological balance, she will not be held responsible for the chaos which ensues. She is the mother of all, but ultimately not concerned with any one race or kind of life to the preference or exclusion of any other.

In her hand she holds the spear, and near the other a sword. To her side we see a blue shield to indicate the importance of the element water in sustaining her kingdom, i.e., all life. The empress has these weapons readily at hand, to act in defense of her realm against those that would despoil it and turn it into a desert. They will bring upon themselves illness, disease, and bad fortune through their pollution of the earth with their chemicals and hormones, their nuclear plants, and their oil spillages.

By the side of her feet we see several fly agaric (mushrooms), potentially dangerous if ingested due to their poisonous qualities, but traditionally associated with the "witches' flight," that is, achieving an altered state through psychotropic substances. Long ago this was an accepted tribal practice, and in some cultures today it is still practiced by shamen and other magical adventurers.

On each side we see the two sacred oaks of Glastonbury. One has died almost completely, and the other lives on. These trees remind us of the Two Trees that gave light to the Undying Lands. They show the balance between the male and female, birth and death, life itself.

TAROT MEANING

The Empress card shows the mighty ability of the earthly plane to create new forms of physical life and support them. She is the sustainer of the material condition. Without her blessing, there is no nourishment, no sustenance, and we her children begin to fade. And not just in an environmental sense; but on other levels also, in particular the emotions. The empress rules over the domain of love, both physical love and attraction, as well as motherly love and a sense of caring. She rules over beauty, especially the beauty of wild places where mortal men find it difficult to go. The spectacular waterfalls, the rock-strewn cliff shorelines, the massive jungles where roads built by men become overgrown again in a matter of days—all are pearls on her great necklace.

The empress also represents harmony, which is the ability to synthesize two mutually antagonistic forces, each opposed to the other's existence. Thus she is able to bypass the mental processes involved in making agreements between contestants, and to use emotion to emphasize those things which they may have in common. She functions on the basis of feeling.

The lives of those in whom the empress is well-developed tend to flow without too many major upsets or complications. Other people respond well to these people; they move smoothly through social situations which some of us would find awkward or embarrassing. They have the ability to make everyone they meet feel good about their situation, and about themselves.

Where the qualities of the empress are too heavily developed, such a person tends to be too compromising, too easily swayed against their better judgment by their surroundings. They tend to concede in situations of duress, especially where they are being made to feel bad about saying no, or when a favor is expected from them. They constantly need to be praised for their efforts, and made to feel worthwhile. Beneath it all is a basic disbelief in their own value, an inability to feel complete without being needed by someone else in almost every situation. In this category are those people who, lacking a life themselves, try to immerse themselves in other people, attempting to find ways in which they can make themselves useful in exchange for a token of gratitude along the way.

ASTROLOGICAL ASSOCIATION
Venus, the planet of love, harmony, and creativity.

The moon rules over the more reactive emotions: reactions to things that other people have done, or emotions which other people might feel. Accordingly, the planet Venus rules over those emotions and feelings which are outwardly directed, that is, not dependent on external stimuli, directed toward others independent of the immediate environment. In mythology, Venus's assistance was often sought to bring people together in a relationship.

But Venus had many aspects, not all of them as courtly as this might seem. She was worshipped in ancient Babylon in the form of Ishtar, goddess of both war and love. Here her role was twofold—she could ignite the flames of love, as well as those of hatred: both extreme emotions have a close connection, united through the level of intensity of emotion that could be experienced at either end of the spectrum.

In the tale of the Judgment of Paris, Aphrodite (Venus) was awarded the prize of the golden apple in a setting which bears characteristics faintly reminiscent of our own Biblical tale of Eve in the Garden of Eden. The golden apple was to be presented to the fairest goddess, and Paris was asked to be the judge. He had to choose between Hera, the goddess of marriage and the home; Athena, goddess of wisdom and battle (especially ingenuity in battle); and Aphrodite, goddess of beauty and love. Paris choose Aphrodite, which naturally pleased her—but brought in its wake problems from the other two!

The story is about the choices we make in our relationships: with whom we choose to have relationships of a more intimate kind and how we handle them. Venus teaches us how to create harmony with others. She makes us see why people fall in love with each other, why we have fallen in love with people in the past, and in the present. She makes us wonder how those who fall in love with us actually see us. Wouldn't it be interesting to get a glimpse of how we are perceived through the eyes of those who love us? Perhaps one day we can actually share some of these perceptions directly with each other!

You see us three sisters here together; three faces of the same energy, and in your lives the force which has brought you into the world and brought you through all the dangers and problems of your early years. We are the women who have brought you into the world, and we will always be your greatest teachers, your greatest challenges, your greatest helpers, and, unless you learn respect quickly, your greatest dangers. It was the thought of his wife at home that kept Tolkien, and many other men, going in the mud of the trenches of the First World War. Sam thought of me as Rose on Mount Doom.

Although it seems as though we are passive, our activity is of a different kind from yours. This is probably how you actually perceive nature and its forces in general: as blind, senseless, lacking in consciousness or self-direction. Each of the elements has its own awareness, and collectively I am the sum of that awareness. But it is not consciousness in the sense that you mortals would understand it. When one of my rivers becomes polluted, or another species of wildlife dies out, I do not immediately react with outrage and drive you all off the planet. Mine is a patience borne of many countless ages of suffering and pain—through having had so many children like you! You are not my firstborn; far from it. I am always bringing new life into the planet. You may not always notice it in the context of your own brief duration of existence, but it does occur over slowly-evolving centuries. If you continue in your present way of pillaging whatever natural resources you find, regardless of the damage you cause yourself and other races, then you most likely will not be here in another thousand years' time. It all depends on how you relate to me.

In another of my capacities I rule over creativity, and that includes the creativity of artists, musicians, writers, and so on. Mine is the inspiration which galvanizes them into action, making them desirous of bringing into being the vision in their heads, staying up all night to finish a promising line of thought, getting it down on paper so they don't lose it. I gave them the ferocity to overcome the cynicism, the criticism, the mockery of others; to be determined to see it through. I am the muse which brings so much beauty into your lives. Imagine if you turned on the radio or television, and there was nothing but quiz games and chat shows. How bored you would soon become with your lives!

Similarly, I inspire men and women to want to have children, to want to see new life be born and flourish in front of them. I provide them with the ability to sustain the life they bring into the world, to feed their children, to care for them and nurture them. Mine is the influence of devotion—but not the devotion of the self-proclaimed martyr. Mine is the perseverance which comes from a joy of giving; a generosity of spirit which does not consider the giving as giving, but rather as sharing and enjoying.

IV THE EMPEROR

Elrond, Lord of Rivendell, is seated at his throne, about to make the important decision of what to do with the One Ring. On the table in front of him lie the symbols of his decision: the One Ring, along with various scrolls and dispatches, implying messages sent by him and received from other emissaries. They denote the worthiness of their holders, in particular the Dwarves, of whom Glóin father of Gimli was the primary representative. The Council of Elrond contained representatives of Dwarves and Elves, Hobbits, Men, and Istari (in the person of Gandalf). For a long time the Dwarves and Elves had been at loggerheads over an ancestral feud. Thus Elrond, who was Half-elven, was an ideal intermediary in this very delicate situation.

Above his head, the ram's horns identify him as leader (ram) of the flock. The ram is the active male principle, and acts with great courage to protect his ewes and maintain his position of hegemony over the flock. Above his throne is the Ring Vilya, the Ring of Air, which is colored blue, the color of the sky when the sun is at its zenith. Growing out of the top of his throne is a tree, symbolic of his association with growing, natural forces, and his positive association with the earth element. The tree is an important symbol showing the link between earth and air: below and above. It draws its sustenance from the earth, yet it breathes up carbon dioxide and pours forth oxygen. Symbolically, the tree is a symbol showing the interconnectedness between heaven and earth; a bridge that makes both realms mutually accessible.

The eight-rayed star emblazoned on the chest of his tunic symbolizes among other things the four seasons, during which would be celebrated the summer and winter solstices, and the spring and autumnal equinoxes. (It was also an emblem used by the High Elves, but with different meaning.) For us, the other four rays can each represent the other four pagan festivals lying between these major dates in the Druid calendar: Imbolc (spring), Beltane (summer), Lughnasadh (autumn), and Samhain (winter). The Elves also celebrated festivals at the solstices and equinoxes. In Middle-earth, the star is the emblem of the House of Fëanor: it represents the Silmaril, made by Fëanor, the greatest of the Elven-smiths. We know the Silmaril as Venus, the Morning and Evening Star.

Across Elrond's left knee rests an arrow, which shows the speed with which he can arrive at decisions and put them into effect. Orbs, representing mercy, are set into the arms of his chair, near to his hand. The two together form the symbol of Mars, the circle with the arrow coming out diagonally upwards at the side.

To one side is his harp, with Elrond's name written in runes along the side of it; the harp is a popular musical instrument among the Elves, associated with masters of lore. Although Tolkien's harps are drawn from the instruments of the medieval bards, the harp is also a symbol in current magical usage. The harp is an indication of the Emperor's association with the creative impulse, expressed through the arts. It is also a symbol which has been used traditionally to represent a hero's forthcoming descent into the underworld, a journey in which the hero confronts his or her greatest fear and makes the great sacrifice of their outer personality (mortality) in order to achieve something of greater magnitude—a place in the stars or amongst the gods through gaining immortality. On another level, the harp is a symbol of the age-old Celtic resistance, in particular, Irish resistance to external rule. The harp in Middle-earth was the instrument of choice for accompanying singing, and thus also represents the oral tradition of storytelling.

During the Council meeting, Elrond follows the gentle process of allowing the meeting to find its own way. He took a back seat, letting everyone speak; and made no attempt to influence the Council's decision-making process. He was aware of the very pressing need for the historic suspicions between Dwarves and Elves to be put on temporary abeyance until something could be done with the One Ring. Elrond shows great humor when he comments on how Sam Gamgee has gotten into the Council meeting, even when he hasn't been invited and his master, Frodo, has. Aragorn reveals his broken sword after Boromir has talked about the message he received in his dream to "seek for the Sword that was broken." This is the famous legendary sword which Aragorn's ancestor Elendil father of Isildur used in his battles against Sauron at the end of the Second Age, and which establishes his hereditary claim to the throne of Gondor. You can imagine that Boromir wasn't overjoyed at meeting a claimant to his own future sceptre!

Bilbo Baggins is also present—he has been residing in Rivendell since his departure from the Shire. He volunteers to be the one to destroy the Ring by casting it into the fires of Mount Doom. This idea is rejected by Gandalf, who knows that Bilbo has neither the resolve to get rid of it, nor the physical strength to make the journey. Frodo then volunteers to be one to continue the quest. He is neither an experienced warrior nor schooled in any of the magical arts. He has no special powers or abilities, at least none that we are told about at any prior stage in the story. What he does possess is a clarity and purity of spirit that reminds us of Galahad, the only one of Arthur's knights deemed pure enough to be shown the Grail and allowed to drink from it. In offering himself almost as a willing sacrifice, Frodo shows his qualities of leadership and individuality.

Elrond suggests that Frodo should be accompanied by eight Companions (matching the Nine Black Riders of the Enemy), and that all races should be represented among them: Aragorn and Boromir for Mortal Men; Glóin's son Gimli for the Dwarves; Legolas for the Elves; Frodo and Sam Gamgee for the Hobbits, along with Pippin and Merry. Gandalf is chosen as the representative of the Istari.

Elrond shows great judgment when he says that the composition of the Fellowship should be based more on friendship than fighting or magical prowess. He knows that these qualities in the end will be needed to secure any victory over the forces of darkness.

The Emperor card is a strong one, denoting the principle of self-determination, the way the individual will may be taken and channeled with an unswerving sense of direction. This uplifts its owner from the rut of personal motive onto a higher wavelength where the good of others is seen as a greater objective. It represents personal freedom, and as we can see from Elrond's style, he is by nature no dictator or despot. He does not need to control every decision that his Council makes. This does not imply a lackadaisical attitude on his part, especially on a matter so important as the One Ring. At the beginning of the Council meeting, it is clear that he genuinely does not know what the best course of action might be (although he has already made up his mind that he himself will not even touch the Ring). He is strong, but he knows his own limitations, and that is the greater part of strength. He allows the strength of others to come forward, to share in his confidence and strength. It is a true mark of leadership when others begin to develop a greater awareness and belief in their own potential and abilities.

The arrow in Elrond's hand shows the ability to move swiftly from A to B, not allowing any blockages to interrupt the flow of action. That which is fired is aimed with accuracy, and should unerringly meet its mark. Our words are like arrows—it is easy to hurt others unnecessarily by sounding off without thought. But in order to be effective, we have to take aim more carefully and make sure that we always hit our target(s).

This card shows the principle of self-help. This doesn't imply an attitude of arrogance, but an experience of greater satisfaction from having totally changed a situation as a result of one's own efforts. This is very much a card of action, showing us how we can effect change in our own lives: no matter how unchanging our situation may seem to be, if we work tirelessly we can begin to make a dent in our seemingly impassable blockages. All we have to do is dedicate ourselves to our objectives, and in the midst of our fury we will have discovered that we have achieved victory. We will probably have our minds firmly fixed on something else at that moment, and the news that we have won will filter into our minds slowly, like a soldier in the trenches being told that the war is over.

ASTROLOGICAL ASSOCIATION

Aries, the cardinal sign of fire, the sign of leadership and motivation.

Aries is a fiery sign, ideal for "getting things done" without delays and without complications. It is a very direct "yes or no" influence, and some people find it extremely refreshing in an age when everyone is going round in circles trying not to offend anyone else. For some, though, Aries can be a slightly abrasive influence in which they feel defensive, mainly because they feel they are being challenged. Aries has an influence of great honesty and openness, yet it hates any kind of external restraint or even questioning. Aries requires that others share the same belief and faith in itself: without that psychological reinforcement it tends to withdraw into a cocoon of defensiveness. It is constantly seeking out new challenges, new horizons, new territories to be conquered. Because of its tremendous faith in life, and in itself, it usually does find such outlets. It is believed that the gods look particularly favorably upon this sign, despite its occasional selfishness and outbursts of bad temper, because it basically means well for the good of all, and generally accomplishes just that.

Aries is a sign of aggression, but aggression isn't necessarily a bad thing. Through aggression—the rightful expression of anger and refusal to tolerate what is not right—we have made changes in society and in our world that would otherwise never have taken place. Against overt exploitation and suppression of human rights, sullen compliance achieves nothing.

THE EMPEROR SPEAKS

I am the Emperor, and I have come to rule this kingdom as a result of my proven ability. My courage has been tested under conditions of great adversity, and my ability to lead and direct others successfully is put to the test all the time.

I have learned the great art of being able to read a person in a moment. I have also learned to motivate people. To encourage someone to do something, not just for his own good but for the greater good, you have to inspire him with enthusiasm. This is a rare quality, but an extremely infectious one.

A greater part of encouraging enthusiasm lies in raising morale. Many people float along with little or no real direction in their lives, waiting for things to happen—things like love, marriage, children, old age, illness, death. Pleasant prospect, isn't it? Well, if that was your philosophy, wouldn't your morale be low? My influence on people is generally to remind them that they are as idealistic as I am, although they may have lost sight of the original vision which once burned brightly in their aspirations. Once they see that, the battle is half won. I give them responsibilities and activities, for there are always lots of things to do in running anything. Whether it's a neighborhood watch committee or a kingdom, it's the same principle.

Morale, I've found, is directly related to level of activity: it has nothing to do with the material conditions of comfort; quite the reverse, in fact. Many times I have led my troops through the mud and hunger of battlefields, only to discover that there morale was at a fantastically high level. Yet when we were sitting around in a secure fortress with all the comforts of a nearby tavern, morale was rock-bottom.

To motivate your fellow creatures, you must give them challenges to overcome. So many people end up in trouble with the law because they are unable to find challenges. In order to solve the problem of crime, you will have to find ways of giving them a purpose in their lives, otherwise their energy will turn inward and become negative. You will have to start taking responsibility—that's right—I said YOU!

V THE HIEROPHANT

The Hierophant is represented here by Saruman, originally the leader of the five Istari (wizards) sent by the higher powers to fight against Sauron, and thus make the balance of power a bit more even. His original title was "Saruman the White," and he was, prior to his incarnation on earth, a Maia (spirit), part of a race of supernatural beings just below the level of the Valar (gods, archangels).

Saruman gained possession of one of the Palantíri—a set of seven seeing stones which enabled one to see far afield and to communicate in mind with others. He undertook a study of the making of Rings of Power in order to combat the One Ring of Sauron, the Dark Lord—and became seduced by desire for it. He looked into his Palantír, and was caught by the stronger will of Sauron. Sauron defeated him in the mental battle, but

Saruman retained the illusion that he could still win. Saruman's ego became hugely inflated, and he sought to gain the Ring, overthrow Sauron, and rule Middle-earth properly. Having summoned Gandalf to Isengard, Saruman suggested that he knew how to use the Ring, and that Gandalf knew where it was to be found. When Gandalf refused to co-operate, Saruman imprisoned him on the top of Orthanc.

Saruman is pictured here surrounded by his magical appliances. His robes are no longer white, but of many colors. He thinks this is an improvement, but in truth he has left the path of purity and wisdom. In his right hand he holds the Palantír he has been using for scrying; it is reminiscent of the crystal ball used by psychics, although from what we can discern this sphere seems to be infinitely more potent. On the pedestal we see a book of magic spells lying open, with symbols of pentagrams and crescent moons written therein. Spears and a shield, symbols of his preparations for war, are to the right, with Saruman's symbol of the White Hand. On our card the hand is shown in the form of a blessing. Hand symbols are used in all forms of mysticism— church practices, Masonic, royal, regimental, even Buddhist.

The jars on the floor show different astrological signs, letters, and again another pentagram (five-pointed star). We can also see instruments Saruman has been using in some of his experiments. The thought chills us—Saruman may be experimenting on his prisoners of war.

He stands on the black-and-white checkered floor, which represents the balance between Light and Darkness in each of our lives. Above his head we see bats flying—these creatures are traditionally associated with darkness and, in particular, vampirism. This suggests that this man's life essence is being siphoned off by some dark power stronger than even he realizes, even as he may be involved in drawing off the life force of his unlucky victims in his dungeons deep below.

TAROT MEANING

You can use the word "hierophant" for ages without really knowing what it means. The dictionary definition is "he who explains." Originally it was the title of the person who appeared at strategic moments in the rituals of Dionysus (Bacchus), god of revelry and revelation, to explain to the participants what was going on. By then they would be well into their fourth day of non-stop revelry, aided by consumption of wine, and (so some historians believe) of other hallucinogenics.

Of course, after days of continuous merry-making, people would be "seeing things," and they would be in a very different condition from when they had started the week-long festival. At one time it was thought to be very prestigious to have taken part in the rites for Dionysus, probably because it was such an intense and heavy experience. The festival began with a troop of people, all crowned with ivy leaves, assembling in a town and moving off into the nearby forest to the accompaniment of music. To give the experience some direction, the hierophant would come out and give certain set talks on what they were going through, on what was being shown to them, and how they could realize more fully the spiritual dimension of their new-found reality. Without his intervention, the whole occasion would have just degenerated into disorganized revelry. In a very real sense, then, the hierophant was a shaman who would oversee the initiation of the members of his "tribe" into an awareness of some of the surrounding realities adjacent to their mundane lives.

Thus the experience would be one of considerable impact, enabling the participants to go away with something more than just reckless abandon. They glimpsed the nature of the causes of things behind the veil or surface level of material reality. Quite possibly they would have experienced the god himself, or at least glimpsed into the gods' realm of heavenly paradise. For the rest of their lives, the stories of their gods and goddesses would seem more real; and they would hold the gods in reverence and respect from then on.

The title "hierophant" acquired new meaning at the turn of the 20th century with the establishment of the Magical Order of the Golden Dawn, a small group of people—mostly academics—who banded together to explore the mystical Tree of Life, a system of knowledge with origins in the Talmudic school of Hebraic mysticism, going back to the time of Moses. The leader of this order was given the title "hierophant," and his job was to learn the rituals and guide the younger members along through the symbolic pathways of the Tree. On these symbolic journeys, the members showed secret signs of acknowledgment (mostly to be seen in the postures of the ancient Egyptian gods on the wall paintings inside the pyramids) and code words ("secret" or Holy Names of God).

The members of the order would also undergo various tests. One such test was for them to be blindfolded and then, after they had been moved around the ceremonial chamber amidst the clanging of cymbals and the smoking of heavy incense, the blindfold would be taken off. This represented their having achieved a higher state of awareness (light). The cymbals and brazier represented the material plane through which they had now symbolically passed, and which they were now able to subjugate to their will. In fact, the hierophant's job was not unlike that of Master of the Lodge in Freemasonry, except in the latter there is no overt recognition of any magical aspects in the ceremonies. Aside from learning considerable chunks of ritual, the personal qualities and integrity of the Master are often put to the test in real life, for he must be able to maintain a sense of harmony and conviviality within his lodge. There is an association of secrecy with this card.

These days we have lots of different types of hierophants making their teachings more publicly available than ever before. We have born-again fundamentalists of different faiths, all crying out for more and more money so that they can go forth and do the Lord's work (just keep paying in, brother/sister). We have all kinds of people promising enlightenment on a weekend away in the countryside, gazing at stones and crystals, or tuning into messages from UFOs. Some of these people are genuine and sincere, wanting nothing more than to alleviate the distress and avoidable suffering of their fellow human beings. Others are not as sincere. Take care when choosing a hierophant of your own.

Another aspect of this card is the tendency to become so stuck in one's traditional ways of doing things that change or improvement becomes impossible. The task of today's guide and teacher is to bring out each student's own "teacher within," so that learning can continue as an on-going process throughout life.

ASTROLOGICAL ASSOCIATION
Taurus, the fixed sign of earth.
This sign represents dependability, honor, reliability, and steadfastness. In times of difficulty and danger, this astrological

influence gives tremendous comfort to one beset by enemies. Taurus's symbol is the bull, which is unyielding and implacable when aroused to anger. Nothing will stop the charge of the enraged creature until the opponent is utterly vanquished, or at least cries out for mercy. This sign is particularly famous for its loyalty to friends and loved ones, and will never desert someone who becomes "special," unless that person is the first one to betray the friendship. But if that happens, the Taurean will not hesitate to break off the connection. Underneath the very powerful exterior is a profound sensitivity and gentleness which tends toward the artistic and creative. There is a basic awareness of the beauty implicit within objects around it: there is a greater awareness of the subtlety of color and texture than with most other astrological influences. Similarly, with music there is a refinement, and a sensitivity for the different textures of instruments and the sounds they can make.

The Taurean influence is second-to-none when it comes to putting that strong shoulder to the great wheel of hard work and responsibility. This sign is capable of tremendous sacrifices if it has a personal stake in the final outcome. It definitely sees its future in terms of creating its own economic and power base, rather than relying on others for a job, a house, etc. Taurus needs ownership in order to feel secure. Ownership confers rights and powers that nothing else can. This sign can tell a troublesome presence where to go, should the situation call for it. Just having that power in reserve means that the chances are that it would never actually be used. The Taurean influence is the embodiment of hospitality. Decorating the home beautifully is of great, almost ritual significance, and the items will be chosen with great care and precision. Only those of the most exquisite quality are good enough. But it is not a flashy presentation, put out to impress you; rather it is an outward reflection of the deep inner spiritual riches over which this sign is guardian. The home is much more than just a place to sleep. It is a place to welcome friends old and new, to entertain—sometimes too lavishly—but the Taurean influence does like to spoil its friends now and again. The repeated buying of tasteful presents is something that can become a bit embarrassing if the recipient feels that they should reciprocate but financially cannot.

The maintenance of cherished memories is important for this sign: the photo album will tend to be a big one, bulging at the seams. The maintenance of traditions is also important for the Taurean influence; not for their own sake, but for the sense of historical continuity which they give, the feeling that some things were the way they are before we came along, and will be even after we are no longer here.

THE HIEROPHANT SPEAKS

They call me Guardian of the Secret Ways, and that is entirely my function. There is nothing that occurs in my secret ceremonies that is incompatible with any religious belief. It is not our intention to take someone away from their faith, but our desire to render that person more useful to his or her society and fellow human beings.

It is true that there are, within our ranks, those from every walk of life and background—not just the well-to-do either, but some who are experiencing great problems financially. Our association is open to any who can agree with its aims and abide by its rules. Our basic desire is to foster the spirit of universal spiritual love between our members in particular, and in our society in general. Now, tell me, how on earth can that be sinister? Only good can come of our association: we do a lot for the needy, motivated by a belief that someone is only as useful as the service they are able to give to those in need. We take no interest in party politics—all that can only lead to fierce arguments and bad feelings; such discussions are banned from any of our meetings, although members are free to believe what they like, or to actively engage in politics, if they so desire.

Our primary teaching is of personal responsibility—we are each ultimately responsible for reshaping our lives, no matter what disaster or tribulations we have gone through at any earlier stage. Now is the time in which we live. The past is there to guide us, but we must not be bound to the past, because that would mean that we would miss our present destiny. The past finds its fulfillment in the present.

There is some truth in the rumor that people can often become quite lucky when they go through our rituals. I've heard various explanations as to why this should be so. One is that there is some intrinsic power or influence which rubs off on the members the more often they do the rituals. Another, more likely, is that when the individual starts meditating on what the symbols mean, then he or she can start coming to grips with the mystery of life, and begin to master it. That is when their karma, fortune, fate, destiny—whatever you want to call it— starts to improve. Obvious now that you think about it, isn't it?

VI The Lovers

The two lovers stand embracing each other, seemingly oblivious to everything else that is happening around them. It is Aragorn with the Lady Arwen, after his victory over the army of Sauron, his efforts aided by the destruction of the One Ring in the fires of Mount Doom. They have been waiting a long time to meet like this. Above their heads we see the symbol of two hearts overlapping, each crimson red, the color of passion and desire. To Aragorn's left is the great sword Andúril he has used in his successful battles (reforged from the broken sword Narsil, which he inherited from Isildur). Immediately behind it is a plant bearing red berries, signifying the sacrifice of men's lives which has taken place in order to secure this victory.

To the left flutter two butterflies, signifying that both Aragorn and the Lady Arwen have become transformed through their love for each other. In the sky above, a flight of skylarks proclaims the end of the period of discord and darkness: now is truly a great time of rejoicing! To the right we see a grapevine growing, although we see no grapes as yet (too early). The hint is that there will be children, the union will be fruitful and continually growing. Beneath this we can see some marigolds, representing the sun (light and warmth) which begins to fructify the kingdom once again now that Sauron has been overthrown. Just to the side of the flowers is a small clump of mushrooms, emblematic of the traditional entryway into the magical kingdom of fairies.

Right at the front we see a beautiful frog, a creature which, like the butterflies, also signifies transformation and development. The frog starts its life as a tiny little creature, and rapidly works its way through a series of differently-shaped designs until it achieves full growth. It makes us realize that the dynamics of change exist in this relationship. And it tells us that love between two people is the most powerful motivating force for metamorphosis on a personality level, and even more deeply on the spiritual level.

Around the two lovers we see a purple canopy, proclaiming the royal nature and spiritual quality of the bond between the two. It is drawn apart as if to give us a glimpse of what these two are up to. For a brief instant we see Aragorn, his head adorned with the Crown of Gondor, and the Lady Arwen, her hair glistening with white jewels, reflecting the awesome radiance of the canopy of stars which gaze down from high overhead. But then, lo! The curtains are drawn closed swiftly by some unseen hand out of sight, and this stage is closed—for us as observers, at least!

This card represents choices which we must all make in our relationships. Aragorn was offered the love of the Lady Éowyn, but knew in his heart that it would not have been right for him to become involved with her. He had set his heart and mind on the Lady Arwen, and nothing could take him away from that resolve. Even more sweet is that which has been awaited with such great anticipation! This card shows us something about our relationships—there are many different forms of love, not just the very romantic version which Aragorn and the Lady Arwen found in each other. Romance is a form of idealizing of the other person and, to some extent, of one's self. Without some idealizing, there could be no attraction toward the other person; it would all seem too mundane, too lacking in zest.

But romance is not the be-all and end-all of any relationship, and a sad fate awaits those who believe it is. They are destined to keep making the same stupid, immature mistakes with different partners, over and over again. For a relationship to work, there has to be a sense of continuity, an idea that the relationship is going to exist far in the future. That future time needn't necessarily be the end of one's earthly days, but the farther ahead it is perceived, the greater will be the life-span of the relationship.

People like friendships that exist over long periods of time. When all else seems to be dissolving into chaos, nothing gives such a sense of security as the familiar face of an old friend or lover whom one has known intimately for years.

A relationship is like a river: it has a life of its own, independent of its contributing influences. Like a river, it will go through infinite changes: sometimes running fast and furious, as in a waterfall, sometimes moving slow and wide as it curves elegantly round a bend. There will be times when the river becomes very deep, and no movement can be seen on its surface at all. At other times it will be very transparent, and it will be possible to see right down to its bottom, and see all the little organisms which contribute to its life force.

Changes in a relationship do not cause the problems between two lovers so much as their refusal to go along with the changes; in other words, their attachment to that particular form in which the relationship has become fixed. A sense of confident detachment is required, a sense of faith that despite the influences of change, the relationship will naturally work out along positive lines. When people feel they are going to lose someone permanently, they become panicky and upset. When that happens it is like losing a major limb, so they say.

In our monogamous society, we make a huge emotional investment when we really commit ourselves to another. Some people like to do this in the context of a traditional marriage, and feel able to commit themselves for the duration of their natural lives. Others are increasingly looking for alternatives, such as private, personalized "hand fasting" ceremonies, in which two people simply go off into the forest by themselves and make a solemn pledge to each other to be loyal and true friends/partners. The man and the woman are facing each other as they make their promises, then they reach out to each other, the man's right hand taking the woman's right, while his left crosses her left hand, both their arms effectively making the sign of an X between them.

This card also gets us to look at what attracts us to another person in the first place. Is it the person, the type, something about them, or the situation in which we meet them? Is it something about the way they dress, the way they move, or talk, or smile? It's all very chemical—or alchemical, really. Attraction is so difficult to define, but there's no mistaking it when it's in the air! Those giveaway body movements, all completely unconscious, that feeling of a rush happening somewhere deep down in the blood. The marvelous way two people's lives begin to merge when a relationship begins!

Fear is the greatest enemy of love—fear of being hurt, fear of hurting another. So many are still carrying the emotional scars of yesteryear's emotional injuries. Being a lover is a bit like being a sportsman—of course you're going to get hurt at some point! Injuries are inevitable! But be proud of the emotional scars you bear; they are the most worthy trophies of your excellence as a devotee of the Goddess of Love!

If you had a child and the child had just started learning to walk, but one day fell over and hurt itself, it would be absurd if your reaction was to tie the child into a chair and never allow it to walk again. Agreed? Well, it's just the same with love—you're going to fall over a good many times before you get the hang of it at all, and even then you're bound to slip on a banana skin somewhere along the line, so you're never going to be completely safe. This is the real world—ultimately, you can't play it safe forever!

People are profoundly motivated to come together via the spiritual dynamic of love; by this I mean each of us has a very deeply-rooted urge to transform and to hasten our own spiritual evolution. Directly connected to our level of consciousness is the nature of our life-state. If we are stuck on the emotional level of apathy, everything about our life will seem pointless. If we are functioning on the emotional level of anger, our lives will be full of battles and fights with others; aggression from neighbors, betrayal from friends, hostility from people passing in the street. By directing our energies in an evolutionary, upward-moving direction, we can reduce our problems in life and hasten our own spiritual evolution into the bargain.

Sometimes we may be drawn into a relationship where, for each person, the spirit within knows that such a love affair is not only desirable but necessary in order to hasten this process of development and transformation. If we are able to bring something of the cosmic awareness and insight into such a whirlwind relationship, then the results can be tremendously liberating. Old patterns resurface, issues you thought you'd dealt with years or decades ago rear their ugly heads, and then go their way with a finality that can't be mistaken for anything else. Such relationships are often karmic, and by that I mean that there is an element of destiny or fate about them. There may be an extremely strong sense of knowing the other person, or of recognizing them from somewhere, of knowing what they are going to say just before they say it. It's lovely when this sense of recognition works both ways. You don't have to talk just for the sake of chattering. Underlying all communication is such a deep set of telepathic images that it becomes second nature for one person to know just how the other feels. It's a bit like finding and reclaiming a lost part of yourself after a long absence.

ASTROLOGICAL ASSOCIATION
Gemini, the mutable sign of air.
This is the sign of the twins, and so touches upon the point just made—the sensation of finding one's "twin," or other half, in this big wide world where such an event seems so unlikely.

When this happens, thank the powers that be, your lucky stars, whatever you believe in out there to be bigger and brighter than yourself.

There is another aspect of the "twin experience," the uniting or bringing together of previously disparate—unconnected or loosely connected—aspects of one's personality. We each have a shadow self—the part of our subconscious mind which contains all our insecurities, all our fears, all our negative or unpleasant (i.e., socially unacceptable) emotions and feelings, everything which we like to keep well hidden and out of sight of others, even ourselves. Here lie all of the creepy things as well—the monsters and the little creatures we used to imagine would run around the bed, the talons of the tree blowing in the wind outside our bedroom window, dark and sinister out there in the blackness.

This aspect of our personality is likely to sabotage our conscious attempts at happiness through loving others. As soon as this aspect gets restimulated—by a situation which in itself is highly emotionally charged—it sets off an emotional counter-reaction which tells us "something is wrong," "the other person is out of order," "this doesn't feel right." It can be any excuse, reason, or justification. But it seems very real to us at the time. We feel panicky, unwell, disgusted with ourselves—or even worse, with the other person—and we have hit the emotional thermostat which tells us that we have had enough love today, thank you. And goodbye. The existence of such thermostats has caused tremendous heartache, most of which was avoidable. Admittedly, we might from time to time need a bit of breathing space; something may have become too intense. It might even be that we do want to finish with someone. All of which is perfectly okay, if that decision is coming from our true selves, and not just a shadow-like tendency toward self-sabotage on the road to happiness.

THE LOVERS SPEAK

We are the Lovers, and in each other's love we have found the greatest fulfillment that we believe exists in this world. All other experiences pale by the light of this one; other forms of attraction seem so shallow, so thin by comparison. We feel as if we have been searching for each other for ages, for countless lifetimes; and now that we are back together, we are going to stay that way.

For those of you who have been hurt in your searching for your lost half, all we can say is keep searching; don't give up. It will all be worthwhile when you find your other half, your soulmate, call it what you will. Until that time, it very often does seem gloomy out there. Some of you may wish to establish other kinds of loving relationships, just until something really significant comes along. At least until then, you can be assured of some love in your life.

The world isn't full of complete wastrels; there are many genuine and caring people out there. You don't have to wait until everything is perfect before you can take the risk of getting involved. Perfection is created as you go along, rather than "discovered" by chance. We bring out the qualities of perfection in those we love. We are the stone cutters, the gem polishers. Ultimately we are only going to get out what we have been able to put in, somewhere along the line. If you feel that you haven't got as much out of your relationship(s), then think again as to whether you're really giving it the 100% necessary to make it go. On the other hand, could you be trying too hard?

Sorry to make you think this way, but we are astrologically connected to Gemini, the twins: it's our job to pose the other side of the argument! Why not just relax a little; calm down. The more you try and push it, the more things aren't going to work out. It could be that subconsciously you're so busy chasing love that by the time it catches up with you, you've moved on to something—or someone—else! Let love come into your life without your putting the stoppages on it, or frightening it away with your own insecurity.

So many people stay on the sidelines because they are afraid of getting hurt. We would laugh if we were to hear of soldiers afraid to go into battle for fear of getting hurt. But it's your duty to get out there and get hurt! Stop cowering on the sidelines. Get off your complaining and open your heart to someone. There must be someone out there who could do with it! You'll find that once you learn to do that, others will actually find you quite a stunning person to be around. I know you don't believe me now, but try it and see for yourself!

VII THE CHARIOT

King Théoden's chariot is careening out from the Hornburg in Helm's Deep. (We have chosen a chariot for its traditional tarot symbolism; in *The Lord of the Rings* he actually rode a horse.) This system of fortifications was the defensive center of the Westfold of Rohan. Gandalf showed King Théoden that he had not just been poorly advised, but actively misguided by his former advisor Gríma Wormtongue (who had been in the service of Saruman all along). Théoden mustered his troops to ride to the defense of the western border, and withdrew to the fortress when Saruman suddenly launched an invading army against him. To his good fortune, Gandalf arrived in the nick of time to expose Wormtongue and warn the king of Saruman's evil intent.

Old King Théoden realized his mistakes, but rallied himself to do what he could to lead his kingdom and his people against the vastly superior army of Orcs, Half-orcs, and Men from Isengard. They resisted the first waves of Orcs, but eventually the attackers scaled the walls and Théoden's guard retreated to an inner section of the fortress. The next morning the ancient horn was sounded and Théoden charged forth, rallying his men and driving the Orcs before him. Gandalf arrived with reinforcements and completed the rout.

After the defeat of Saruman, King Théoden led his Riders to the aid of Gondor. They arrived in the nick of time, just as the Witch-king had broken down the gates of Minas Tirith. Théoden was slain when his horse fell upon him, but his niece Éowyn (who had joined the army in disguise) and Merry the Hobbit killed the Witch-king.

This card shows Théoden charging the Orcs, representing both battles. Théoden was old, and fell into his dotage, but recovered to lead his people to victory in their darkest hour.

TAROT MEANING

This card represents the ability to remain focused on those things which are really important, to keep one's concentration on where one is heading and not get sidetracked by the insignificant or the trivial. It requires considerable strength to be able to pull the reins of a chariot, especially if there is more than one horse. In this picture, Théoden has just one horse hitched to his chariot. He cuts a commanding figure, leading his small army of devoted soldiers to fight the overwhelming odds arrayed against him.

The chariot is also about the fortitude to go it alone, if need be; it challenges the automatic, conditioned notion that unless other people approve of what we are doing, we should start to doubt ourselves. It's hard to go against the herd instinct, no matter what we may consciously espouse. This stems from ancient times when it was infinitely risky for one not to belong to a tribe or grouping. One of the worst punishments a tribe could impose on you in those days was that of being kicked out of the stockade. Outside that little row of sticks were bears, wolves, ferocious humans, and who knew what else? How could one go out and get food all alone? It would take a team effort to catch any substantial animal; humans are not that fast on foot, especially over rough countryside. Sleeping alone was another problem; when the sun disappeared below the horizon, all kinds of strange spirits moved through the darkness. The entire world completely changed its personality.

This card also gets us to look at our barriers, our protective shields behind which we find it safer to operate than if we walked into situations completely open and vulnerable. In an ideal world, we would never need to test the virtue of those new people with whom we meet and associate. However, in the real world we need to very much, so one of the aspects of this card is the element of caution in our dealings with others. Here, trust is earned over a relatively extended period of time; it is not so easily given away in the vague hope that it won't be betrayed.

The chariot is an instrument that enables its driver to move quickly from one spot to another with the benefit of some degree of protection around his sides. We all want to protect ourselves and our families from danger; as society continues to pose more dangers to us, there may be an increasing trend toward people pooling their resources in order to live in very small, easy-to-protect compounds, not unlike the stockades of our more distant ancestors. Inside of these, it will be possible for one's children to play undisturbed without fear of danger. Families would come together, in the sense that the elderly will live in the same compounds with their grown-up children. Here they can safely enjoy what they have worked all their lives for: the chance to see their children and grandchildren growing up. If carried to extremes, however, the protective walls we build around ourselves can become a prison.

ASTROLOGICAL ASSOCIATION

Cancer, the cardinal sign of water.

This is the sign of caring, of looking after, and of nurturing. Its glyph is the crab, which moves around safely inside the protective confines of its exterior. Its shell gives the crab the freedom to move around safely; without that it would have to be a better-camouflaged creature. When confronted with danger, the crab waits in its shell until the intruder gets bored and goes away in search of easier prey. The essential symbol, then, is the barrier in which the crab lives and protects itself. The crab also tends to move sideways, causing some element of confusion in the mind of a potential attacker; it represents the ability to do the unexpected and throw any predator off balance.

Cancer is the symbol of the mother (as is the High Priestess in another, slightly different aspect) through its connection with the moon, and so also is the Moon card, in another slightly different way. Here, the mother is shown as wanting to create a safe space for her offspring. This is such a deep primal urge that many men can't quite grasp it, especially if they haven't had children themselves. Without that feeling of safety, parents can have no confidence in the society in which they live.

A negative aspect of the Chariot card is the inability to bring things to a point of completion. In a spread of tarot cards, a reversed (upside-down) Chariot card tends to have this meaning. It indicates that the querent (the one who is having the reading) makes a habit of starting things and getting into them a bit, but never really finishing them off. For instance, the querent might begin a course of study, but never get to the point where they are able to put it all together and make sense of it. That is why it is so important that any course of training consists of an equal balance between theory and practice. Without that balance, the student tends to want to give up, and if prevented from so doing, will become increasingly antagonistic at school and prevent others from learning also.

THE CHARIOT SPEAKS

I am the Chariot, and you meet me here at this point in your quest now that you have mastered the lessons of both the Hierophant and the Lovers. The Hierophant introduced you to the orthodoxy of formal training; while the Lovers showed you how to get in touch with your feelings, your emotional spontaneity. Now you must integrate the two. I use two reins to drive my horse; the rein on the left symbolizes the receptive feminine, while that on the right symbolizes the active, masculine side. It is by a controlled use of both of these forces that the chariot maintains its forward motion and doesn't topple over. Too much of either force could spell disaster, especially in an emergency. If I were to topple over, I would be pounced upon by Orcs and almost certainly be killed!

VIII STRENGTH

The White Tree of Gondor is surmounted by seven stones at the bottom and seven stars at the top. The White Tree (named for its white flowers) was a descendant of the tree planted in Minas Tirith at the beginning of the Second Age. By the time of the War of the Ring it had died, and no seedling could be found. But Gandalf knew of a seedling growing in the mountains; after the final defeat of Sauron, Gandalf and Aragorn brought the seedling back to Minas Tirith. It began to grow again, sprouting little white buds, symbolic of a new age of harvest (i.e., the beginning of the Fourth Age).

The tree is an ancient symbol which links the spiritual heights with the earth below; when looked at in its bare essence, the design appears the same on the upper and lower portions of the tree. In *The Lord of the Rings*, the new tree was a sapling. We have depicted it as more fully grown in order to emphasize the "summery" theme of this card (its astrological association is Leo), rather than the "springtime" association of the sapling.

Significance of the Tree as a Symbol

The tree is an important symbol in mysticism. With its roots deep down in underground waters, its trunk the pillar of the material world, and its branches reaching up into the heavens, it symbolizes the Cosmos. Because it stands vertically, the tree represents the male principle, and is the *axis mundi*, providing shelter and shade, nuts and syrup, fruit, and protection from the storm. It also symbolizes the nourishing power of the earth goddess. Trees have long been revered as deities, or at least the dwelling place of spirits or doorways to the presence of a deity.

In ancient times, many temples were simple groves of trees, the doorways of which were formed by the trees themselves, while the altar would be a rock or stone before the greatest tree. Later on trees were knocked down to build temples of stone, but even when this happened the tree motif endured. Reflected in the stained-glass windows of Christian churches is the same principle of diffused sunlight, as if filtered through foliage.

In India, the Buddha achieved enlightenment after sitting under the bodhi tree. In Greece, the laurel was sacred to Apollo, and the willow to Artemis, while Zeus's tree was the oak. In Arabia, spirits were said to inhabit the trees and thickets. In their forest groves, the Celtic Druids, literally "men of the oak," held meetings and performed rituals and sacrifices. The Norse god Odin hung upside-down for nine days and nights from the World-Ash Yggdrasil in order to gain the runes. Jesus was crucified on a "tree." The Tree of Life in the Garden of Paradise offered two fruits, enlightenment and immortality, while the Serpent of Wisdom coiled around its trunk. In its most developed form, the tree is the Sephirotic Tree of Life in the Holy Qabalah. The Tree of Life maps out the many pathways which lead up through the range of human experience back to Union with God.

Trees are key in Tolkien's writing, also: the two Trees which gave light to the Undying Lands; their descendant, the White Tree of Gondor; the golden mallorns of Lothlórien; the evil Old Man Willow; and the Ents and their Trees which attack Isengard. There are also several forests throughout Middle-earth.

Significance of the Seven Stars and Seven Stones

The number seven is echoed though the number of stars in the heavens above and the number of stones embedded in the earth below in the form of a circle. In astrology, before the discovery of the three outer planets (Uranus, Neptune, and Pluto), there used to be only the seven so-called "holy" planets. There are seven notes on the musical scale (the eighth is actually the first note played again, but this time on the next scale up). The Jewish Menorah has seven branches, while the initiation cave of the old Roman religion of Mithras had seven doors, seven altars, and a seven-runged ladder for each of the seven grades of Initiation.

Noah's ark landed in the seventh month, and the dove was sent out on the seventh day. We also have the seven deadly sins, seven pillars of wisdom, seven days of the week, the seven seas, the seven visible stars of the constellation Great Bear. There are seven chakras, energy centers located within the human body, running parallel with the various glands, from which certain powers begin to emanate once these centers are opened through meditation and chanting.

The group of standing stones laid out in the form of a circle around the tree links us to our ancestral past, gently chiding us to remember that without our past, we all would be effectively uprooted, leaving it only a matter of time until we should dry up and wither away. We should all honor our ancestors, or at least acknowledge them, if the word "honor" is a bit too strong.

The two interlaced squares represent the process of manifestation. The square is a symbol of that which has achieved a balance between earth, air, fire, and water. The second square, though, immediately suggests that the harmonic balance of the elements is not a static and unchanging condition. It is a fine balance that to some extent is self-adjusting, although should the elemental scales tip too far in the direction of any one of the elements, the balance would be very likely to be permanently upset. Say, for instance, that there were a massive case of radiation fallout, a huge nuclear reactor exploding without warning. This would tip the balance too strongly in favor of fire. If the polar ice-caps melted, and the water level rose by a corresponding 30 feet or so, huge areas of land (earth) would simply vanish. We would find ourselves occupying a small fraction of land mass, with a greater proportion of the planet's surface now functioning as sea (water).

Interlaced through the branches of the White Tree is the zodiacal sign of Leo, the curling shape resembling the mane of a lion, which represents courage and self-esteem.

Seven is a very powerful number in mythology the world over. There are said to be seven stars in the constellation Pleiades, or the Seven Sisters as it is sometimes called. This constellation can be seen by the naked eye at night very close to Taurus the Bull. The Seven Sisters were nymphs, daughters of the Titan Atlas, and were pursued so vigorously by Orion that the gods changed them into doves and set their images in the stars. In Tolkien's tales, the emblems of Gondor and the King had seven stars and a White Tree; Elendil brought seven Palantíri (seeing stones) from Númenor; and there were Seven Rings for Dwarves. The White Tree was a descendant of the White Tree of Númenor, descended from one of the Two Trees which radiated light in the Undying Lands. The number seven shows completion, the culmination of all the other influences into one single focal point. It suggests the principle of "as above, so below." In other words, as it is in small things, so it shall be in greater things.

TAROT MEANING

This card has seen a number of different versions in the last 200 years. Originally, in the Visconti-Sforza, the Marseilles, and in the Swiss 1JJ decks, the Strength card suggested mere brutal physical power, the kind that overwhelms and is capable of breaking limb from limb. This was undoubtedly the general conception of strength in those days, and the card showed Hercules fighting with the Nemean Lion, and just about to hit it with his club. A strong, but nonetheless quite brutal expression of strength and power.

It wasn't until the early 20th century with the publication of the Rider-Waite deck that we saw in Pamela Colman Smith's design a far more gentle expression of strength. A woman, with an infinity symbol hovering above her head, gently—without any apparent effort on her part whatsoever—either opens or closes the mouth of the lion over which she stands so regally. The symbol is clear in that it shows the dominion of reason, or possibly even the spirit over the physical passions of anger, desire, lust, and so on. Waite was the first to switch the traditional placements of the Strength and Justice cards in the deck. Strength became the eighth Major Arcana card, Justice the eleventh. Waite's reason for doing this, never made totally clear, probably had to do with the neatness with which all the cards would fit into the sequence of the astrological signs and planets.

Aleister Crowley, in putting together his Thoth tarot deck, maintained his own individual style perfectly in re-titling this card "Lust," and replacing it back into his deck as the eleventh card, switching the place of Justice (Adjustment) with Strength. Crowley objected to Waite's swapping the placements of the two cards, and so took them back to their original placements. There was no deep mystical secrecy going on behind the scenes, only the colossal egos of these two rather spiritually undeveloped and arrogant individuals.

True strength comes not just from big muscles. I have seen really big, strong men cry and fold up like babies when confronted with real tests to their inner strength. True strength has to do with the personality, and involves one's ability to stand fast to what one believes. It involves courage, grit, determination, and a refusal to lose sight of the objectives you have set for yourself. Very often guys who have relied all their lives on physical size or muscular power find that when the chips are down, they haven't developed the reserves of character and persona which would give them the ability to bounce back after a negative condition or occurrence. This sense of resilience is not achieved on a weekend workshop or at night school. It can only be cultivated over time, through developing a pioneering, adventurous attitude, and by facing adversity with a certain cheerfulness.

The design of this Strength card represents a radical departure from the Pamela Colman Smith/Waite version, which emphasized the "reasonableness" and almost genteel quality of the Christian influence which Waite brought to his mysticism. Here we have shown a new conception of Strength, namely, that of the White Tree, refusing to be beaten under by the forces of Darkness, constantly re-sprouting itself to begin the long and arduous struggle of growing again into a great and mighty tree. The tree illustrates the idea that resilience comes from renewed growth.

This card is a guiding image for this new historical phase into which we are entering. It shows that our real strength is achieved by aligning our own earthly lives (the stone circle) with the powers of spiritual growth (the stars above). The tree stands as the bridge between this world and the higher (or adjacent) dimensions, showing that our growth is dependent on a balanced intake of each of the four elements: fire (in the form of light), water (emotional happiness), earth (material security), and air (purification of thought processes). If there is an insufficient amount or an excess of any of these elements, the tree within each of us will not grow and develop as it should. If there is too much fire, we will become dehydrated and eventually burn out. I have seen this many times with psychics and people that continually operate at a very high pitch. If there isn't enough fire in your life in the form of inspiration or hope, you just won't be able to fully function on any level. If there is too much water in the form of emotional intake, you will become "soggy," a "damp blanket"—but if there is an insufficient amount, you will dry up and become emotionally paralyzed. If you have too much earth, you will become heavy, and if not sufficiently rooted into the earth element you will not be able to "hang on" to your foundations and become easily uprooted. With an insufficient intake of air, you will become stuffy and claustrophobic to be around. With too much air, you will become detached and cold, overly intellectual, and out of touch with your emotions.

The tree within you is the connection between the higher spiritual forces which are guarding this planet and the earthly plane. Your tree is connected to every other tree within every other person, just as ultimately each actual, physical tree is connected ecologically to every other tree.

ASTROLOGICAL ASSOCIATION
Leo, the fixed sign of fire.

The qualities represented here are those of amusement and recreation, and the strong drive to experience life as a celebration. Those in this sign will desire to enjoy themselves and the material things which life may bring, but will have to accept heavy responsibilities in order to do so. This will contradict the free-spirited nature of this energy. Themes of love, recognition, and children—either the children one has or one's own "inner child"—will cast themselves into that person's existence. Life's learning will involve being at the center of attention.

The lion was the symbol of the tribe of Judea, and it was inscribed on the tribe's banners as it led the Children of Israel through the desert. This tribe consisted of the most determined fighters, the champions of the people.

The ability to provide a safe space in which the talents of others can grow will be called upon. Such people may find challenges in their paths, but they will exhibit their greatest potential out of love for others more often than out of love for themselves. It is not enough to achieve; one must incorporate achievements into one's personality and make them a part of one's personal growth.

It is important not to get so wrapped up in one's achievements that one cannot surpass them with higher expectations and greater objectives. The energy of this symbol is a great heightener of hope and aspiration.

Leo's regal presence in one's chart imparts a style which is positive, warm, and playful, possibly even dominating. Such an emphasis may not be fixated on the physical realm of activity, but toward the more unusual realms of experience, transforming those powerful energies toward uplifting spiritual awakening. Compulsiveness, jealousy, and control may have to be resolved. Pride can act as a blockage, but real nobility is often in showing oneself on the same level as another person and not being "puffed up."

STRENGTH SPEAKS

I am your new symbol of strength, replacing the previous representations which had kept you trapped in so many of your old patterns of conflict and contradiction. I am here to show you how you can become strongly rooted into your earth, so that you can draw sufficient nutrients and water into your life in order to bring you happiness. Without sufficiently wide and deep roots, how can you hope to become able to draw enough happiness into your life? Happiness is like a food supply; it feeds the emotional body, the astral body. Without it, you become haggard and unwilling to face the beauty which each new day can bring. You have the natural ability to turn your leaves toward the light, the down-flowing force of spiritual illumination which emanates to us from the angelic realms. The light guides us in our knowledge of what is right for us to do in our lives.

The stone circle around me functions on many levels. It is a filter through which the cosmic energies from above can become more closely integrated with the energies of earth, as they begin their process of emanating out through the ley-lines of the planet. The stones also shield me against the more harmful negative energies which might make their way to where I stand—negative energy fields such as those that emanate from electric cable lines, or where the earth energies have been blocked by construction work (erected without any consideration or awareness of how these developments cut across the particle flow of energy through the ground).

As you can see from the very tips of my branches, I am linked with the farthest stars, reminding you that you humans live in a very interconnected universe, and that it is now only a matter of time before you receive more and more visits from other life forms throughout the galaxy. Up till now, you have been rather like the inhabitants of a South Pacific island, far out from any contact with other cultures.

The melting of the age-old barriers between the realms will expose you to new dangers which you have never before had to deal with. You have been protected from some of the more negative forms of life in other realms by what you have perceived as the angelic realm; increasingly you will have to find ways of looking after yourselves. You must resolve your inherent tribalism, and develop a sense of family that transcends religion, belief, and race. None of these challenges will be easy.

IX The Hermit

Tom Bombadil, holding his lamp, makes his way through the great forest. He has stopped by the stream of life, and looks into it very thoughtfully. Tom is one of the most ancient spirits, and has existed from the time that Middle-earth was formed. He is the primordial spirit of nature, and has no interest in the petty squabbling between any of the races of Middle-earth. The feather on his hat is a symbol of truth. Tom stares into the distance, deep in contemplation. He isn't looking for anything in particular, at least not on the physical plane.

TAROT MEANING

The hermit is a symbol of solitude, of withdrawal from the hustle and bustle of everyday life to a point where one can begin to filter out all the noise and find an inner voice of truth. This card is connected with places of meditation, such as retreats, ashrams, monasteries, and so on, where people can go to get back in tune with themselves and begin to see their lives from a fresh perspective. In such places they can reflect seriously on life and receive a source of guidance that comes from a very deep place, instead of just acting on impulse. In the lives of saints and holy people—Moses, the Buddha, Mohammed, Jesus, and other such figures from spiritual traditions the world over—there is always a time in which they remove themselves from society to clear themselves in order to be able to receive fresh inspiration from Above.

It may be difficult for you to relinquish all responsibilities and take a retreat, but the more difficult that is, the more you obviously need to do it, even if it's just for a short time. We each empty our physical bodies regularly of physical waste matter, and would become ill very quickly if we were unable to do so. Similarly, we must be able to empty ourselves of the emotional and psychological debris we collect from our interactions with our environments and other people. Stress is a serious problem in modern life, and the hermit shows us the way of dealing with it. When we are unable to actually retreat off into the countryside, we should at least make it a point to go for a stroll in a park or by a river. Even for an hour each day, we can unload much of the negativity that affects us and connect with the cleansing energies of nature.

Practices such as meditation, yoga, and visualization are also under the domain of this card. In his hand, the hermit holds the spiritual quality of realization which lights his own path and stands out as a beacon for others to follow, if they so desire. But he isn't a guru: he is very different from the hierophant, who does have this function. The hermit is too busy working on his own issues to want too much involvement with other people and their egos. This card also relates to the hermetic tradition, the yoga of the West, which incorporates the studies of the tarot, astrology, and alchemy.

Inverted, this card indicates that the querent feels a sense of isolation or alienation. It shows a desire to go off and digest some of your experiences, whereas in the Fool card there is a sense of optimism about exploring new spheres of experience. Experience has taught the hermit to be watchful where he treads, to look at the path that unfolds before him, and not to step out so blithely and trustfully into the world. This card also relates to the value of silence, through which we find the chance to clear our minds of chatter and allow the voices of our inner selves to communicate more audibly with the conscious mind.

ASTROLOGICAL ASSOCIATION

Virgo, the mutable sign of earth.

This sign is very much concerned with purity and authenticity. It has a sharp eye to look out for any shortcomings, and is critical and attentive to detail. The Virgo mind is analytical, constantly asking "why." Virgo is associated with health, both physical and mental.

The Virgo principle is attached to details as well; it has an awareness that there is more to successful ventures and results than just looking at the overall picture. After the overall picture is made, it has to be broken down into smaller fragments so that people can be assigned their individual responsibilities and tasks. This sign has an awareness that small is large; that little things can influence the outcome of big things. Virgo is able to anticipate and prepare for the unexpected eventuality.

Virgo is a sign that does not necessarily open itself all at first meeting; it will instead reveal itself over a duration of time and maintain a reservoir of emotional fuel that will sustain any ensuing relationship. This sign knows that nothing comes with an unlimited supply, and therefore gradual usage should be made of any resource. This is one reason why this sign has a connection with the environmentalist movements. They perceive that the natural resources of this planet—forests, oceans, water, the food chain—are all being subjected to extreme pressure by the exploding world population, and by humankind's decimation of the planet's ability to create new resources.

THE HERMIT SPEAKS

I am the Hermit, otherwise known as Tom Bombadil, and you find me here in my natural setting. I love my forest—all of nature in its wildness is my domain, all places where it is possible to be alone, to get back in tune with the earth, the water, the seasons. Why do so many live in cities? Those places originally came into being when your society became fixated on manufacturing, and vast numbers of people herded into them to find work. It was a convenient way for business owners to store their labor force, enabling them to call upon any number of surplus workers when they needed them, and dropping them off when they didn't. But now those times are over. As the old age of industry passes into history, so will the economic need for cities, and bit by bit you will find opportunities opening up to free yourself from their magnetic pull and escape into the country-side. Those that remain will be those who are happy to live under conditions of what will become jungle warfare.

Attend to your need for periodic purification, physically, mentally, and spiritually. Those of you who think you can go through life continually absorbing new spiritual practices as if you were one big black hole have a very mistaken idea about the actual path to spiritual awareness. You must continually "excrete," and drop off whatever you don't actually need. For many of you that will involve leaving behind previous teachings and teachers. For others it will involve dropping off other kinds of dead wood (including friends or associates) where there is no sense of anything of value occurring in your interaction.

For those of you who don't meditate, let me advise you to take up this practice. In a sense, you are each meditating right now, although not consciously. To meditate, all you need to do is become aware of the nature of your thoughts, emotions, and reactions to people that you meet, situations that you come across, and things that you see. The best way into meditation is to become an observer of yourself—this way you will quickly develop that sense of detachment and clarity of vision that meditation brings. Gradually you will begin to emanate that special aura that will make people approach you as if you have the answers to their existence. When this starts to happen, simply be aware of what your feelings are at that point. The real road to spiritual growth lies not in suppressing these feelings, but in not acting upon the ones you instinctively feel are wrong. There is no "should" or "shouldn't" about feeling the way you do, only in the way you choose to act.

X WHEEL OF FORTUNE

The Wheel of Fortune is depicted as the One Ring. It made men mad with lust to own it, to possess it. Those who did possess it generally lost all power of independent thought—they became servants to it, caretakers of it, lost in the illusion that they were gaining access to vast powers. The greater they believed themselves to be, the more they were under the spell of the Ring. It was forged by Sauron in the fires of Mount Doom, the great volcano which lay in the north of Mordor. He made it in order to bring all the other Rings of Power under his dominion.

At the top of this picture, on the left, is an encircled septogram (seven-sided figure), representing the Seven Rings forged for the Dwarves. In the middle we see three interlaced circles, representing the Three Rings for the Elven Kings. One is white, showing Nenya, the Ring of Water, owned by Galadriel. One is red, for Narya, the Ring of Fire borne by Gandalf. The third is blue for Elrond's Ring, Vilya, the Ring of Air. On the right we see an enneagram, a nine-pointed inter-linked design that represents the Nine Rings which were made for Mortal Men, which were distributed by Sauron to key rep-resentatives of the human race in order to control them.

At the bottom of the picture we can see the Noldorin Elven-smiths of Eregion hammering into being the Rings of Power. They, sometimes with the collaboration of Sauron, created the Rings of lesser power. All, except for the One Ring, consisted of a single band of metal set with a gem.

The Elves of Eregion experimented with making magic Rings. Sauron came to them in disguise and learned their secrets. When Sauron had taken in all he needed to know, he returned to his land of Mordor and forged the One Ring. The Elves then knew they had been betrayed. Sauron made war on the Elves, and captured the Seven and the Nine: Eregion was laid waste. Sauron was eventually defeated and returned to Mordor. The Seven Rings given to Dwarves did not enslave them, for Dwarves cannot be dominated, but the Rings did increase the Dwarves' lust for wealth. The Rings given to Mortal Men were successful; they faded away and became wraiths. Sauron took back their Rings and they were forever under his power. The Elves were willing to lose the power of their Three Rings in order to destroy the One.

On the One Ring we can see the inscription:

Ash nazg durbatulûk, ash nazg gimbatul,
Ash nazg thrakatulûk agh burzum-ishi krimpatul.

translated as,

One Ring to rule them all, One Ring to find them,
One Ring to bring them all and in the darkness bind them.

These words were spoken by Sauron when he put on the One Ring. This inscription on the One was visible only when heated by fire. The writing is a special mode of Tengwar in the Black Speech, the language of Sauron.

TAROT MEANING

The Wheel of Fortune shows the ups and downs of life, how we mortals desire success, and all the trappings of material well-being. We seek, if not power, then certainly control over our own lives. For some this search is obsessive; nothing else matters. The desire for fame, money, and recognition can become all-consuming, making everything else seem unimportant. Some have approached the wheel with a sense of the inevitability of rising and falling in terms of the fortunes of human life; but it actually contains teachings which, if applied, enable you to achieve abundance and maintain it as well. Once the level of success is achieved, the wheel is there to advise a certain element of restraint and moderation. When people become overly optimistic in their anticipation, they set themselves up for a let-down. This applies on both an emotional level and a financial or business level. People who speculate too heavily when the stock market is on a massive upswing see their bubble burst, then stand to lose everything, perhaps even their homes and basic standard of living in addition to the initial investment.

The wheel also represents the principle of cheerfulness, especially in the face of adversity. In our ability to bounce back from any of life's negative circumstances, we show our real faith in ourselves. Belief in oneself, or even in the natural ability of the universe to care for and support us, is a basic quality which gives us the courage to take a chance and commit ourselves to a situation in which the final outcome is unclear.

This card has a special link with all that lies outside the range of our immediate environment, and comes up in spreads to represent foreign travel or associations with people from overseas.

Negative aspects of this card pertain to an inflated sense of self, arrogance, and the belittling of others through invalidation and indirect carping. The wheel is also related to our individual ability to "bounce back" from any of life's negative or difficult conditions, and to retain good humor in the face of adversity—this is one of life's greatest challenges. The reversed Wheel of Fortune card can show the bursting of the proverbial bubble when high hopes are broken with bad news.

ASTROLOGICAL ASSOCIATION

The planet Jupiter, symbol of faith, hope, and affirmation.

Jupiter is known as the "greater benefit" and under the more traditional astrological approach was thought of as creating nothing but good. In fact, this planet does induce life to flow more easily and under this influence whatever you do seems to work out well.

This planet shows growth—the individual reaching out to experience more around themselves. Jupiter has a strong social aspect as well, representing the law, the legal system, and people in power—a function which it shares with the sun.

It also represents the highest ideals of your life; those things which you believe in and hold very dear. The influence of this planet can be a consciousness-expanding one, as the material aspects of life can become actually less significant than they were before.

Even if material success isn't attained under this influence, it still brings benefits of a more intangible kind, particularly the feeling of learning and developing new abilities which previously were unrealized or dormant.

THE WHEEL OF FORTUNE SPEAKS

Many are those that chase after me, but I bestow my favors upon those whom I deem worthy. Yes, I have a mind of my own, and would slip from one finger to another if I felt the time had come to move on from someone who was keeping me out of circulation for too long. Gollum had me for ages, under that mountain in the darkness, and when Bilbo came along I saw in him someone who was going to bring me out of that little cul-de-sac and back into the mainstream of life.

I can bestow certain powers upon whom I will, but I do so in accordance with that person's natural level of ability. With Gollum it would have been pointless for me to have given him the power of vision: all he wanted was to sneak around and spy on people, catch fish, and be invisible.

I will always bring out a person's greatest ambition. Look at Boromir, who dreamed of becoming king, the greatest warrior in history. Such overweening ambition, unless backed by a very strong practical reality, can be the undoing of many. One can have an optimistic vision of how life can be different; but it is another matter entirely to put one's own ego at the very center of everything. Even Frodo, standing at the edge of the Cracks of Doom, was unable to make the final act of renunciation and cast me into the abyss.

Mine is the power to motivate people through all manner of hardships and suffering. Without that vision, without that desire, or the belief that dreams could actually come true, people would just sink into the mire of apathy and live quiet, boring lives of resignation and mediocrity.

Above me you see the other Rings of Power that were forged before I came into being. When I was created, I absorbed and mastered all their power. As the Three Elven Rings represent each of the three elements (air, water, and fire), one might interpret me as the Ring of Earth, giving the others expression into reality. The Seven Rings for the Dwarves could show the seven levels of the universe, now given meaning by my existence. The Nine for Mortal Men each represent one of the Spheres of the Mystical Tree of Life, while I represent the Sphere of Malkuth, the Kingdom: the world where all these other dimensions begin to come into focus and reality.

XI JUSTICE

The Oathbreakers of Dunharrow are summoned by Aragorn from their kingdom of shades to pay back their debt for breaking their oath to Isildur, Aragorn's ancestor.

Aragorn looked into the Palantír and saw a fleet of Corsairs sailing from the south. He needed to pass into the south quickly, and took the Paths of the Dead, the haunted passage under the mountains. These paths were haunted by the ghosts of Men who had sworn to aid Isildur against Sauron, and reneged. Isildur cursed them so they could not find rest until they had fulfilled their Oath. Aragorn, as heir of Isildur, encountered the Dead in the passage, and summoned them to fight against Sauron. Their appearance on the battlefield frightened off the Corsairs who had been drawing up from the south. Thus the Oath was fulfilled. Upon the retreat of the pirates, Aragorn held their debt repaid, and permitted them to go back to the realm of the dead and find peace.

TAROT MEANING
This card is about the payment of karmic debts. What this means is that each of us does things in life that we later regret, or feel we have to justify. Our inner self knows that these things are wrong, and that somewhere along the line a price must be paid for them. We may not realize it when we repay these actions, or we may have lost sight of any association between the cause and the effect of the problems experienced later in life. When these problems build up, we can become overwhelmed. Ultimately we are each responsible for the karma we incur. It is admittedly difficult to see what we or someone else might have done to deserve something bad that happens to us; in fact, there is no "deserving" about it, in the sense of righteous judgment from some deity figure. Rather, through taking responsibility for ourselves, we are able to gain control and consciously redirect the path of our lives.

Responsibility level is related to knowledge. For example, in the area of personal health: increasingly, people are moving away from the notion that they should delegate all responsibility for their health to those in the medical field toward an awareness of nutrition, the need for exercise, fresh air, and water. Any area of life has the level of knowledge connected to the level of control. Power without control is nothing; it represents a condition which is almost definitely going to go wrong at some time, and that is when someone's power will work against them.

This card relates to the clearing of karma through looking

back over scenes in one's life where one has acted less than optimally. This can be painful when one realizes the emotional impact their actions have had on others. Now is the time to atone for regretful choices we have made. The Justice card also represents the results of our actions. Jesus said that "by their fruits we would be able to judge them," meaning it is not by someone's words that we can get an effective picture of them, but by their creations and their effects on others.

The Oathbreakers, in a sense, reflect our "past lives." When the reactive mind is open to suggestion (as via hypnotism), one "goes back" to enact a scenario where one is an archetypal hero, warrior, villain, beguiling maiden, royal personage; whatever comes up as an image to work with that clears a blockage from the querent's life. The scenes can be thought of as archetypally, if not historically, true. Whatever expresses itself as a "past life" is another aspect of our personalities, a projection of thought-form onto the blank screen of our lives. Thus, in a very real sense, what you see is what you are.

Negative aspects of this card include lack of balance, unwillingness or inability to reach a compromise, and difficulty in a partnership where any long-term commitment is required. The reversed Justice card can show the querent's search for an ideal relationship. In a spread, it could indicate a see-saw effect of "in love, out of love," a continuing roller coaster of an affair that is actually going nowhere. Learn to step back and truthfully assess what is going on, what your mistakes are, and what you are learning.

Libra, the cardinal sign of Air.

This sign is connected to the principle of balance, and by implication, harmony. It is the quality to enable any force to find its equal and opposite, and thereby become reconciled to the harmony of that which encompasses it. When it appears prominently in the astrological charts of people, it shows their basic desire for partnership in life.

Libra also connects with artistic and cultural potential, as there is a sensitivity toward the emotional undercurrents implicit in situations; there is a refinement of temperament which can connect with other people's needs in a way that is light and unobtrusive.

JUSTICE SPEAKS

We are the Oathbreakers, summoned here by Aragorn, the rightful heir to the king whom we betrayed. We took the oath of allegiance to him, but did not fulfill it when he needed us. We have suffered long enough in our kingdom of shadows, in the Dwimorberg, waiting for an opportunity such as this to clear our debt. You see us here having finished our mission: Aragorn has just told us that we can go back and trouble no one ever again. Ah, the bliss of liberation from our dismal existence! Let our experience be a reminder to you never to betray the bonds of your loyalty, lest you live your lives in the shadows of regret and remorse. Always act according to the dictates of your conscience.

XII The Hanged Man

Denethor, the Ruling Steward, favored his son Boromir the warrior over his other son, Faramir, whom he scorned as a "wizard's pupil." Faramir had a chance to take the Ring, but failed to do so, which greatly angered Denethor. Faramir, having been seriously wounded outside the walls of Minas Tirith, and equally wounded by his father's rejection, is lowered onto the pyre by Denethor.

Faramir is shown in the traditional tarot position, hanging from one foot: one would not treat a wounded man this way! Nor was the pyre burning yet in the story. Faramir was unconscious and Minas Tirith was under siege; Denethor looked into the Palantír and, betrayed by Sauron, believed all was lost. In his despair, Denethor prepared to burn both himself and his son before the Orcs could break through the walls and overtake them. Gandalf, summoned by Pippin, was able to save Faramir, but Denethor immolated himself.

The White Tree of Gondor is seen in the window beyond, the squares in the four corners of the picture represent the four elements: light blue for air, dark blue for water, red for fire, and green for earth.

TAROT MEANING

This card shows suspension of activity; an experience or moment when things may suddenly stop and come to an abeyance. In those moments it is possible to get a different perspective of what is going on before we continue on with any particular course of action. Such times are important crossroads in our lives.

Many ancient legends give an account of a man or god who is suspended upside down, in particular Odin, who hung upside down from the World Ash Yggdrasil for nine days and nights in order to learn the secret of the runes and obtain them. Christ was also hung upon a version of a tree—a wooden cross—in a slightly different version of sacrifice. This card often comes up in the spreads of those who tend to give away their own power to the other person or people in their lives, yet another form of sacrifice.

Sometimes in life we are stopped by circumstances beyond our immediate control; we must wait for bureaucratic processes to be completed, or exercise patience so that others may catch up with us. We may not be ready for what we need to learn and experience in life, and we have to take time out to further our training, sharpen our skills, improve our qualifications, or prepare for the next step. What we do with our periods of waiting very often determines the outcome in the energetic periods that follow stagnation or inactivity. Those who have made good use of their time and resources, even minimally, will have increased their potential for success or survival more than those who sat idle. Our children need us to teach them the value of time, and the importance of making good use of it, for time is truly irreplaceable.

ASTROLOGICAL ASSOCIATION

Neptune, the planet of dreams, ideals, and illusions.

This card is associated with water. Neptune was the name of the Roman god of the oceans. He was the ruler of the oceans, and of all the life they contained. Neptune (Poseidon) took offense at Ulysses (Odysseus) when, during the sacking of Troy, Ulysses smashed the statue in Neptune's temple. In punishment, Neptune prevented Ulysses from reaching home for years, by sending fogs, mists, illusions, and diversions to bar his way, as told in *The Odyssey*. Thus this planet rules over all that can mislead us. Neptune also has an association with drugs of all kinds, and with liquids, especially alcohol, as these have the same effect of creating illusory states of beauty in the minds of their consumers that cannot be perceived by others who are not under the same influence. In *The Silmarillion*, the Vala Ulmo, Lord of Waters and King of the Sea, intervenes in the affairs of Middle-earth.

The planet Neptune is associated in its most positive aspect with artistic and creative inspiration, even spiritual enlightenment. Its particular vision is the reality that "we are all one." In its negative aspect, Neptune represents escapism and the refusal to confront and deal with reality.

THE HANGED MAN SPEAKS

I am the Hanged Man; my life is dangling quite literally by a thread, as you can see. Beneath me is danger, but I am unaware of it, as inside my own reality at this time I am many miles away from all of this. I got into this mess through being wounded outside the walls of Minas Tirith, leading my men to safety. My father wanted me to be more like my brother Boromir, the warrior. My father did not approve of my actions: I let the Ring go; my brother would have taken it for him. We parted in anger, and I am filled with grief.

Now I hang suspended in time and space, not quite in this realm, and not yet in the next, passively awaiting what my outcome will be.

XIII Death

The card shows the battle between Gandalf and the Balrog on the Bridge of Khazâd-dûm in the Mines of Moria. The Balrogs were originally spirits who had served Morgoth and become evil. They were mostly killed off before the Third Age, but this particular Balrog remained hidden deep in the mountain until roused by the Dwarves while mining for Mithril. The Balrog then drove the Dwarves out of the Mines, their home.

The Balrog was also disturbed by the Companions of the Fellowship during their journey through the Mines, but the Company was able to make it to the far side of the bridge before it was upon them. Gandalf battled with the creature, repulsing it with the power of his staff, breaking the bridge; but the Balrog's whip wrapped around Gandalf as it fell and took Gandalf with it. Gandalf killed the Balrog, and then he too died; but he was sent back as Gandalf the White to fulfill his earthly mission. Thus, there is no death, no finality. In this scene, Gandalf—who has come to Middle-earth, the realm of mortals, from higher in the spiritual hierarchy—comes face to face with the Balrog, which is a symbol of a similarly ancient life force but coming from deep within the bowels of the Earth itself. What comes from above meets with what comes from below. It is implicative of the confrontation of the archetypal hero with the dragon, or Minotaur, after having made it through the labyrinth or underworld.

Tolkien was deliberately vague about the Balrog's exact image—which is part of the Balrog's terror. It is also the terror of death itself—not knowing in what form it will appear. The main point, however, is that the Balrog and its weapons are fire, the whip is lightning, the mane is tendrils of trailing fire.

Above the picture is an hourglass—the scythe is the symbol of time and splits the image between death and rebirth. The hourglass itself represents the limitation of time which we mortals find ourselves up against. The symbols of both Scorpio and the egg are present; the egg represents rebirth and new life just about to move from dormancy to activity. The eggshell is a reminder that new life cannot be attained without breaking up old patterns; and that which has been traditionally a source of comfort and protection must at some point be sacrificed to make way for our growth. The skull represents the transitory nature of this lifetime, and reminds us how brief and sweet is life's embrace. So quickly are our opportunities presented to us and then whisked away, we don't always know enough to make the most of them. The ammonite shows life's spirals, and how we move through an evolutionary pattern; even the DNA code has a double helix pattern when viewed microscopically.

Contrary to popular supposition, this card does not mean physical death when it comes up in a reading. What it does show is the clearing away of negative conditions in order to make way for more positive ones that are due to come into the querent's life. The Balrog symbolizes the aggressive and unconscious desires of life; Gandalf in this conflict shows the directing power of spiritual awareness over the lower faculties of mind and body.

Some of the more medieval tarot designs picture the grim reaper, with scythe in hand, cutting down human life in the same way as grain would be cut down by a farm laborer. In medieval times death was potentially near at hand with the most minor of mishaps. A small accident, which these days would require nothing more than penicillin and a bandage to fix, would then involve amputation of limbs and probable death. If your house burned down, there would be no insurance company coming along to help you back on your feet. If someone killed you, there would be no police service that would be able to investigate the crime and chase the people concerned. Life then hung by a far more precarious thread than we can fully imagine today.

The egg is the universal symbol of space and time, with all creative potential within it, breeding all life. The egg symbol appears in legends from Fiji and the Far East to Greece, Egypt, Scandinavia, and Central America. In Hinduism the egg was laid on the primeval waters by the Divine Bird, and the Three-Face god Brahma hatched from it. In ancient Egypt, the egg laid by the Nile Goose hatched the sun-god Ra, and Ptah; and Kneph the serpent produced the egg from his mouth, symbolizing the Word, the primordial vibration "Om." In ancient Britain, the Druids held that the serpent's egg was the foundation of all life;

in Orphic belief the egg represented life, death, and resurrection. The egg also represents the soul in other traditions.

ASTROLOGICAL ASSOCIATION
Scorpio, the fixed sign of water.

Scorpio represents intensity and passion, and is closely connected with sexuality. It represents the ability to transform, to undergo a metamorphosis, to shed one physical mode of existence and move onto another—just as a caterpillar moves on to its next level of existence by becoming a butterfly. It loses just the trappings and limitations of the lower level of existence as it develops greater powers and the ability to move.

This sign is also very involved with wanting to find things out, with searching beneath the surface level of reality in order to find out what is taking place on a fundamental level. Those for whom Scorpio is prominent in their charts will often feel an urge or prompting to seek out something that remains hidden, which may involve a journey into the hidden depths of the mind. In this deck, that experience is symbolized by the journey of the Company into the Mines of Moria.

The descent of the hero/heroine into the labyrinth is an archetypal one: recall Theseus, in the labyrinth to confront the Minotaur, aided by the ball of thread; and Persephone, snatched down into the underworld by Pluto (Hades), Lord of the Underworld, only to be allowed later on to make a periodic return to the surface level of earth; and Orpheus's journey to bring back his deceased Eurydice using a seven-stringed harp to charm the guardians of the underworld. Egyptian mythology tells of the journey of the dead souls, led by Anubis, through the underworld to where they are weighed in the great scales.

There is also the legend of the death, dismemberment, and resurrection of Osiris. Jesus Christ's descent into the underworld after the crucifixion where he preached to the souls of the dead is a continuation of the archetype.

DEATH SPEAKS

I am Death, and I stand here at this point in your quest to see who amongst you really lives up to everything you claim about yourselves. Only the most worthy pass my tests. The illusions I can conjure are the most powerful that you will experience in this lifetime. Only those among you who are able to set aside your fixed reference points will be able to embrace the greater realities over which I have dominion. For a seed to take root, it must first of all die a little death, and then it is ready to become something far greater than it would have been otherwise, had it remained where and what it was. Every winter you see Mother Nature die a kind of death: centuries ago, to your ancestors, it seemed as though the world around them was dying. Death is really a form of sleeping, and in winter all that is happening is that the world is breathing out. In spring, it is breathing in again.

As you have seen from some of the legends already recounted, every hero/heroine must pass through my initiation in order to become more complete. The Egyptians especially realized the relevance of regeneration; every day the great serpent Apep would rise to do battle with the sunboat of Ra, be killed by Set, and be dismembered by the Cat-god Bast. Yet during each night—the period of "death"—Apep would regenerate itself and rise in the morning, ready to fight again.

XIV TEMPERANCE

Frodo and Sam sit with Gollum, having captured and subdued him by forcing him to "swear by the Precious"—that is, to take a solemn oath on the Ring which Frodo carried. Frodo would not actually reveal the Ring lest it drive Gollum mad.

Here, they debate the wisdom of their choice. Sam is clutching his blade, thinking it would probably be better to do away with Gollum on the spot. On our card Frodo holds the Ring in his right hand, pondering over his actions. Frodo is telling Sam not to kill Gollum for the sake of pity—and because they may need him later. Sometimes the most unlikely people and situations can be our best guides and teachers. To remove Gollum at this point would be to deny the natural order of the world.

Above their heads, water is poured from one cup to another, showing the tempering of human experience which leads to wisdom. Water evaporates, then condenses in the air, to reform as drops of rain, which in turn go through the same cycle again. This process represents the refinement of the human soul through successive incarnations, coming back to the earthly plane to be refined, to learn more, and then move on again into the other-worldly levels.

TAROT MEANING

Looking into our past experience enables us to learn more effectively in the present. The word "temperance" has, in this context, little to do with the societies which campaigned for the abolition of alcohol in the early part of this century. Rather it has more of an association with the hammering of a sword on an anvil, in order to temper the steel, to make it strong.

In some representations of the Temperance card, artists have depicted an angel to indicate the influence of the higher spiritual powers on events here on the earth plane. In this tarot deck, we have left out the angel, because of the extremely indirect and minimal support which those powers actually give to humanity. Higher spiritual powers, represented in *The Lord of the Rings* by Gandalf and others, do not continually intervene in the story and come to the aid of the good guys whenever things start getting tough. In this way we are given a reminder that we cannot relinquish our own responsibilities in confronting evil by simply calling upon the higher powers to intervene and solve all our problems. We must rely on ourselves to confront and overcome the challenges we face.

In some tarot decks, the angel is pictured looking into a pool of water from above. This represents the principle of reflection, of consideration being taken before action. This is precisely what we have shown in our version of the card: Frodo and Sam think very carefully about what they are going to do before embarking upon it. Temperance is balancing action with judgment in order to take the best course.

ASTROLOGICAL ASSOCIATION
Sagittarius, mutable sign of fire.

This is the sign of freedom, of being expansive and adventurous. Those with this sign prominent in their charts will want to explore new horizons and go places, both actually and mentally. They will tend to be open to new ideas, and have a very good connection with those who operate on a philosophical level, who believe in what they are doing. This sign is connected with openness and generosity of spirit.

TEMPERANCE SPEAKS
I am Temperance, and my function is to enable each soul to evolve and refine itself. This happens through listening to that still, small voice within.

Good fortune can often come disguised. In this scene, Frodo restrains the initial impulse to rid himself of Gollum, and instead is opening himself to the possibility that Gollum's appearance on the scene might actually be a stroke of good fortune. One of my key purposes is to refine character in the face of adversity!

XV THE DEVIL

The ill-spirited Gríma Wormtongue is sitting in his study, poring over ancient magical books of knowledge to gain more powers which he can use to control others. Carved on the side of his throne is the astrological sign of Capricorn. A dragon's head hangs above him; in this context it is emblematic of greed and conquest. As we look at Wormtongue's chair more carefully, we see that it is in fact a siege machine, used for throwing things over city walls—the concave of the chair being the place where objects such as barrels of burning oil, rubble, or the carcasses of dead animals would be placed to be catapulted into a besieged city.

As we look at the dragon's head, it seems to turn into a horse, the symbol of Rohan, the kingdom where Wormtongue was King Théoden's advisor. This shows us his ability to give the appearance of advising the king for the good of his kingdom, while all the time preparing for the king's downfall.

Across the floor we see some of the artifacts he uses to direct events in this kingdom. There is his quill and ink stand, for writing out orders; and the globe of Arda, which would inspire him to dreams of glory that would further be encouraged by Saruman. On the globe we see, on its right hand side, the outline of Middle-earth; while on the left we see that of a western continent. Wormtongue's dreams of conquest obviously include this western continent as well; once he has mastered enough of Middle-earth, presumably he will want to go about constructing a great fleet of ships in order to sail across the Western Sea. On the floor beside his scrolls we can see the word "Riddermark," the Rohirrim's name for their land.

Originally Arda was flat, with the continent of Middle-earth in the middle, the Undying Lands to the west, and an unnamed continent to the east. Mortals were forbidden to come to the Undying Lands. Númenor was in the sea between Middle-earth and the Undying Lands. The last king of Númenor, Ar-Pharazôn, was driven by Sauron to seize immortal life by invading the Undying Lands. Then Ilúvatar (God) intervened, the Undying Lands were removed from the world, and Númenor sank beneath the waves and became Atalantë, the Downfallen (the parallel to Atlantis is deliberate). The world contracted upon itself and became round. The eastern continent is now the New World. Here we have Wormtongue dreaming of conquering the western continent, and perhaps of sailing to the Undying Lands beyond the world.

Above Wormtongue's head, where the ceiling ought to be, we see the stars shining at night, but here the night-sky is bathed in a red glow, suggestive of the state of war and upheaval into which this man's politicking is about to plunge the kingdom. By his side are various spider webs, implicative of the webs of lies and deceit that are the tools of his trade. A doorway is placed at the end of the room, with no apparent door or handle—only complete blackness, representing the realm of darkness into which his activities open. Above it, as this Devil's own personal hallmark, we see a triangle with a red dot in its center, symbol of manifestation.

There is a trap door, which apparently leads down into a lower region, an underworld of some kind. Although there is a ring on the outside with which he can open this door, the texture of it is still pure blackness, for it is a cosmic doorway to another realm of darkness. Behind the chair is a railing which holds up some of the mechanism of this big chair. This suggests the aspect of pulleys or little wires which connect some very different realities, a representation of something like the Internet.

TAROT MEANING

The Devil card represents negativity in all its forms. It shows deceit, misrepresentation, and the absence of truth. It represents our own need to be careful who we listen to, who we select as our representatives and leaders, and in whom we trust with power outside the realm of our knowledge and control. King Théoden trusted Wormtongue, and as a result nearly lost his kingdom. Wormtongue was "turned" by the convincing words of Saruman into one who would undermine Théoden and persuade him to permit unchallenged passage of Orc raiding parties through Rohan, and to imprison his nephew Éomer.

Wormtongue was a victim as well as a perpetrator of deceit.

He believed that through serving Saruman he would be able to attain greater power, thus assuaging his own inferiority complex. Wormtongue desired the Lady Éowyn, in addition to other privileges, once Rohan fell. He was a little person who dreamed of becoming greater, but lacked the potential to achieve greatness. Wormtongue, driven mad by Saruman, killed him and ran; he was killed in turn by the Hobbits. Thus he met his destiny.

ASTROLOGICAL ASSOCIATION

Capricorn, the cardinal sign of earth.

This sign is associated with achievements, material success, and power; its symbol is the goat. The goat is responsible for the devastation of what used to be incredibly lush areas of vegetation in the world: Iran, Afghanistan, what is now the Sahara. Wherever it was kept as a domesticated animal, the goat stripped all the bark off the trees and ate all the roots of the vegetation, thus removing the base of the food chain.

In Biblical times, a "scapegoat" was used to ritualistically send away the sins of the village. The sins were placed on the head of a goat, which was then sent out of the village, to "purify" the karma of the inhabitants. This card therefore also represents our tendency to blame others for our own shortcomings and negativity. It is easy to point an accusing finger in some other direction: the government, the opposition party, or any other grouping based along religious, racial, or ideological lines. This card suggests that instead of laying blame on others, we look to our own inability to take responsibility.

Because of its prominent genitals, omnivorous appetite, and bad smell, the goat is sometimes used to symbolize lust, and physical appetite in general. The Roman satyrs were depicted with the horns, legs, hooves, and genitals of the male goat. Even today the satyr represents the male sex drive, and we use the word "horny" to refer to lust. Christians, who took a dim view of unbridled sex, transferred the attributes of the satyr to the Devil. In some tarot decks, the Devil is shown with goat attributes, seated upon a throne, holding a man and woman captive as a consequence of their lustful choices. In this card, lust is directly connected to power.

The goat can be very destructive when allowed to roam free, but it also gives us milk, meat, and hide, without which pastoral people could not survive. The physical appetite is necessary for our survival as a race, but if allowed to go unchecked it can destroy our spiritual well-being. This card reminds us that we need to keep our physical and spiritual aspects in balance.

J. R. R. Tolkien was born under the sign of Capricorn. Capricorn's energy is excellent for enhancing survival. They tend to grow up quickly and look after their younger siblings, both of which Tolkien did. Capricorns also tend toward the opposite quality: when they reach a ripe old age of 80 or 90, they tend to become youthful and almost revert back to the excited energy of childhood. People born under this sign, or who have a substantial influence of it in their charts, work hard and wait long for those rewards which they know take long years of service and dedication to achieve. Often there is the sense of one or even both of their parents being absent, even if only for a while. Capricorn influence is oriented toward the long-term future and the benefits that lie there. To the Capricorn mind, nothing worthwhile is achieved without a sacrifice of some kind.

THE DEVIL SPEAKS

Go on, blame me for all your own shortcomings! Anything to avoid the responsibility of making your own decisions and standing by the consequences of them.

I have been here amongst you in one form or another since the beginning of time. Outside of yourselves, I would appear as the negative conditions of nature which would decimate your crops and your villages, like an earthquake or tornado. I would also appear in the form of attacking soldiers from other tribes, unexpectedly charging your homesteads with ferocity.

Within yourselves I represent the need you have to become stronger, and to overcome your inherent laziness and self-satisfaction. Without my influence you would never have a motive for going beyond your limitations. I will always be around, in one form or another, to spur you on to greater things.

In another of my aspects I represent sexual blockages and the problems which can result from them. People with these difficulties will often not even imagine that they have such problems—they will continually place their focus on some other area of life. But when these problems can be overcome, then many other things which previously have not been working out can become unblocked.

XVI THE TOWER

Isengard is being destroyed by the Ents, who rip out the walls of Saruman's castle. Positioned on the battlements of his castle we see some of the great machinery for which he was renowned: a great wheel and a series of pistons. Parts of the castle are on fire, caused by some of his experiments being disturbed in mid-process. Around the rim of the card is a representation of a castle, seen from above; the individual towers are shown in red, and the wall is shown by the interconnecting black line.

The Ents, who are the shepherds of the trees, represent the force of nature against the man-made structures which seem so powerful as they loom above humanity, threatening dehuman-ization and alienation. The tower may be intended as a refuge, but it can turn into a prison. Saruman was imprisoned in his Tower of Orthanc in Isengard by the Ents, who had destroyed it as a possible future power base.

This card also represents anger, as here we see the Ents wreaking their vengeance on Saruman for the destruction of their forests. Anger is not always a bad thing, but it must be expressed positively in order to create a change in society. We should not remain quiet on those issues we feel strongly about; we should speak out so that our feelings and opinions can be registered.

Sometimes the structures that we build for our own safety are the very structures that limit us in life, while true freedom is only found when the inner journey begins. As Jesus said, "And ye shall know the truth, and the truth shall set you free." For as long as we cling to our shadowland reflections of the Great Architect's plan, we can never help rebuild the symbolic temple of initiation in our own lives.

The tower as a symbol is seen in Genesis, with the story of how men tried to build the Tower of Babel so high that from its summit they could launch an attack on heaven. They were able to proceed well into their work, as they all spoke the same language. In order to confound their project, Yahweh cursed them so they all started babbling in different languages, then split into seventy hostile nations and scattered over the face of the earth.

Others feel that the tower symbol is a parallel with the fall of Atlantis, where, "in a single day and night" 10,000 years ago this continent was supposed to have been destroyed by earthquake and flood. Some believe that Stonehenge and the Pyramids were built by the Atlantean civilization, or at least some remnant of it. The story first appears in Plato's *Timaeus:* Sais, Plato's ancestor, was visiting the Egyptian capital when he was told by a priest about a huge continent west of the Pillars of Hercules (the Straits of Gibraltar) from whence all civilization was derived.

Some have located Atlantis in the mid-Atlantic, others place it in ancient Troy, or even Crete.

Occultists such as Max Steiner and Madame Blavatsky developed the theme in their writings. Many from spiritual backgrounds such as these believe that old souls from Atlantean times are being reincarnated even today, bringing with them the tremendous knowledge and power needed to bring in a new era.

Tolkien also incorporated the story of Atlantis into Middle-earth. Númenor was an island in the Western Sea inhabited by Men of great stature and wisdom. But they grew proud, and their last king, Ar-Pharazôn, invaded the Undying Lands to seize immortal life. The Undying Lands were removed from the world, and Númenor sank beneath the waves. A few Men remained faithful to the Elves, and led by Elendil of the royal house, escaped to found the kingdoms of Gondor and Arnor in Middle-earth. Aragorn's ancestor Isildur was the son of Elendil.

TAROT MEANING

We need to build on solid foundations in all our undertakings, moral, ethical, and organizational; this requires planning everything properly before we start anything major. It is no good getting halfway into a project only to realize that you haven't got the resources to complete it.

The Tower is shown in various decks as being struck by lightning. If the people who built the tower had had the good sense to put in a lightning conductor, they would not have experienced the disaster! But they prefer to blame God or nature, rather than to take the necessary action to avoid or avert the problem in the first place.

Towers are interesting symbols. Historically they have been used as observatories to study the movements of the heavenly bodies. These movements are taken as portents for certain kinds of action, such as the planting of crops, official engagements, even marriages. There is a negative aspect to the phenomenon of towers, though—even in our everyday lives.

When people in power make decisions about our future while looking down from their high towers, it is easy for them to feel "god-like" and distanced from the humanity they are supposed to serve. Staying in a tower cuts people off from others, so that they do not have a sense of direct control over their environment. They lose contact with the earth energy and become alienated and lonely. The creation of these types of towers has caused the destruction or effective imprisonment of communities. The tower can also represent the distance between academics and the outer world; the "ivory tower" has become a byword for the realm of intellectuals.

Negative aspects of this card show a lack of safety, care, and attention. The struts or supports which hold one's life in place sometimes feel unsturdy or altogether absent: there is a feeling of having worked hard to build up a life, only to find that one is still hanging in mid-air, wondering whether one will stay in action or fall. Anyone can potentially fall from grace by doing something totally out of character, or by suffering a false accusation that ruins one's reputation.

ASTROLOGICAL ASSOCIATION

Mars, the planet of energy, action, and power.

This god was the father of Romulus, the founder of modern Rome, who, with his brother Remus, was raised by a she-wolf.

Mars was an agricultural deity before he became a god of war. The sacred spears and shields of his cult were kept on the Palatine Hill in Rome. His assistance was invoked before any major military campaign, and sacrifices were offered to him before and after battle. Mars would always be given his share of the booty, as well.

When this planet features prominently in someone's astrological chart, it signifies the qualities of decisiveness, leadership, and courage. Another positive aspect of Mars is the quality of discipline, which the Roman army used to good effect on the battlefield. Negative aspects are violent or cruel tendencies.

The color of Mars is red—for blood and for fire. Fire is an important association, as it is used to forge the weapons of war which may in turn obtain victory. The metal of this god/planet is iron, which the Romans used in their swords, spears, armor, and shields. Iron proved to be much more effective than the bronze used by other neighboring civilizations which the Romans went on to conquer. Iron is still used in forging weapons, as it is the base metal for the creation of steel.

THE TOWER SPEAKS

I am the Tower, and I occur in your lives as an experience to challenge you. When everything is going easy for you, your mettle is never put to the test; but when you encounter me, you begin to realize who your true friends are. Friendships forged in times of danger are solid bonds.

Within my walls you can imagine the fear and panic of the inhabitants, seeing the protective walls of their lives ripped away as the advancing armies move into their homelands. In order to survive you will always need protective devices or boundaries like me around you, otherwise those that intend you harm will succeed. On a national level, you will need a boundary to prevent your homeland from being stripped of what it has of value, with nothing put back into it. Even on a psychological level, you will need to preserve the integrity of your space.

I am here to remind you of the value of remedial action, before disaster strikes. Most calamities can be avoided with a modicum of foresight and common sense. Disempower the irrational and ignorant, and the selfish interest groups which support and finance them, before they drag you into calamities for which everybody pays.

XVII The Star

In this picture we see the spirit or the light of Nenya, the Elven Ring of Galadriel. Nenya is the Ring of Adamant, meaning certainty. The helmet is a symbol of mercury, the winged messenger. The card's basic meaning is hope, which Galadriel always held.

Above Galadriel is the star Eärendil, blazing with twelve rays of light extending into the universe. In her left hand she holds a jug, with the sign of Aquarius inscribed on the side, which she used to fill the basin of her Mirror, and from which water flows down to Middle-earth. Galadriel's Ring, made of Mithril, could only be seen by those with special powers. For instance, Frodo, as the Ring Bearer, was able to see the Ring on Galadriel's hand when she took him to look into her Mirror. The Phial which Galadriel gave to Frodo contained the light of Eärendil captured in the water of Galadriel's Mirror.

Stars were extremely important in Tolkien's mythology. The word "el" means both "star" and "Elf"; the Elves were the "people of the stars." The Elves awoke under the stars, before the creation of the moon or sun. (The order of creation is the same as the tarot deck: stars, moon, sun.) Elendil means both "Elf-friend" and "star-lover."

Eärendil bears across the sky the last remaining Silmaril (the one captured by Beren and Lúthien). Eärendil is Venus, the Morning and Evening Star. Tolkien's inspiration came from the Old English poem "Crist":

Eala Earendel engla beorhtast
ofer middangeard monnum sended.

or, translated,

Hail Earendel, brightest of angels
above the middle earth sent unto men.

Here Earendel refers to John the Baptist, who presaged Christ (certainly a symbol of hope!) and also Venus, the Morning Star, presaging the dawn. The quest of the Silmaril is described in the Queen of Coins.

The goddess symbol used here is a feminine archetype of the guardian of humanity—the two trees that lie in the background of the more traditional tarot designs are shown here as two pillars, from the tops of which emerge the green flora, the life of the world. The two pillars are symbols of the Two Lamps of the Valar, destroyed early in the First Age. When the construction of the world was complete, the Valar (creating spirits) decided to light the world with two Lamps; one in the north, the other in the south. Morgoth, the spirit of darkness, overturned these lamps, sending fire across Middle-earth. The Valar then withdrew to the Undying Lands, which were unharmed, and created the Two Trees, one of which radiated silver light, the other, golden light. These Two Trees represent the principles of masculine and feminine, not competing or contending with each other but each enhancing the other's beauty. The lights of the Two Trees were combined in the Silmaril.

TAROT MEANING

The Star represents hope and inspiration for all humankind. It epitomizes the qualities of peace, serenity, and tranquillity, and how these qualities are attained when we are able to rise above the limitations of traditional thinking and embrace a greater sense of cosmic consciousness. It inspires us to think above our own situations in a way which embraces humankind as a whole, and encourages us to hope that we may be victorious against the forces of Darkness.

Other versions of this card picture the Seven Stars of the Pleiades. Some believe this constellation to be the source-point of a high level of spiritual inspiration, the home of numerous cosmic beings that are currently channeling energies of healing and understanding which are beneficial to humanity. There are also said to be other energies emitted by beings from other constellations which are inimical to our positive development. The Pleiadians battle these beings from time to time. Some say these actual experiences are the origins for all the stories of wars in heaven between gods and demons, angels and dragons, etc.

These are wars which are going on here on earth as well as above, to this day, both within ourselves and in our societies.

Eccentricity and originality are vital themes of this card; reversed, it reminds us to keep focused on long-term objectives.

ASTROLOGICAL ASSOCIATION

Aquarius, fixed sign of air.

This is the sign of humanitarianism, the symbol of the new era we are approaching. It symbolizes new knowledge, inspiration, and a shift in consciousness away from the age-old tribalism and hierarchical systems of the past. This sign has a link with new forms of thinking in every way: new technology, new scientific advances, and spiritual patterns come under this heading.

The ruling planet of this sign is Uranus, which is the planet of originality and eccentricity. This makes Aquarius the sign which breaks down barriers and walls; sometimes literally, as in the case of East Germany. Uranus formed a very powerful aspect to its natal chart, and the Berlin wall, one of the greatest symbols of oppression the twentieth century has known, has been broken down.

Those who have Aquarius strongly in their charts will tend toward a certain ability to be detached, and for them the path of spiritual unfolding will certainly involve developing a sense of not being so emotionally involved in situations.

THE STAR SPEAKS

I am the Star, sometimes called the Star of Hope, always here in the night sky whether your plans work out or not. I am here to give you encouragement when you stumble and end up going through the Tower experience yet again.

I will teach you the value of maintaining a perspective, of not allowing yourself to get too emotionally tied up in your present turmoil. When you have developed this sense of perspective, other things will naturally take their own place in a new ordering of your lives. This new ordering is going to happen on a world level, so it would be good for you to embark upon it yourself, letting its influence into your own existence as much as possible. The more we as individuals can do to pave the way for the New Age, the more harmonious will be its advent.

I am the source of inspiration you reach for in your periods of greatest darkness, when it seems as though there will be no end to your troubles and setbacks.

XVIII The Moon

Shagrat and Gorbag, the two Orc Captains responsible for the capture and imprisonment of Frodo, are in front of the Tower of Minas Morgul/Minas Ithil. Minas Morgul was the name given to Minas Ithil—the former means "tower of black magic," while the latter means "tower of the moon." It was renamed after the Ringwraiths captured it and made it their home. The walls of Morgul shone with a pale, frightening light.

The scene also represents the watchtower on the other side of the pass from Minas Morgul, where Frodo is imprisoned. Sam used the Ring and the Phial of Galadriel to pass through the defenses to get inside and free Frodo. The two Captains are talking about what has happened in the underground tunnel in the pass where Shelob dwells—they have seen the slashed web and are discussing the uneasiness of their Silent Watchers over the last two days. They are aware that something is up, but they cannot see what that might be. Their suspicions are aroused, and they give the alarm to their troops that vigilance is called for.

In the sky above we see the phases of the moon. Immediately above the tower is the dark phase of the moon, indicating the complete absence of light—clouds from Mount Doom cover the sky. At this point in the story, it seems almost impossible that the heroes will be able to pull themselves through. Yet immediately to the left of the darkened-out orb, the new crescent moon shines through, showing that after a period of darkness, the light inevitably comes.

TAROT MEANING

Deception, people being misled. In the story, Frodo and Sam have both been misled by Gollum into entering a long dark tunnel where the giant spider Shelob dwells. Gollum told them that it was a way into Mordor; the Companions soon discovered they had been betrayed by Gollum, who wanted the spider to destroy Frodo and Sam so that Gollum could regain the Ring.

This card also represents illusion, and the influences that can cause someone to forget their real path in life. Sam maintains a good grasp of his mission, and keeps a sense of realism about how he can go about freeing Frodo from the bonds of the enemy. Reversed, the Moon indicates that you will believe what you want to believe regardless of the truth.

The different phases of the moon also remind us of the beginning, middle, and end phases applicable to any human situation and relationship; even an ending can be a new beginning for a new phase in a relationship. Tolkien took great care to represent the phases of the moon accurately in *The Lord of the Rings*.

ASTROLOGICAL ASSOCIATION

Pisces, mutable sign of water.

Pisces is associated with the psychic realm, with sensitivity, and with the ability to pick up thoughts and impressions from the minds of others. The symbol of Pisces is two fish tied to each other by a thread from each of their tails. It hints at the attachments which this sign can form, generally for its own good, but often to its detriment.

There is a quality of dreaminess about this sign, an other-worldliness which makes it a bit hard for people with Pisces prominently in their charts to keep their feet on the ground. Connected with this sign, though, is an amiable quality, a kind and loving streak which earns them the affection of many. The most strongly negative characteristic of this sign is its tendency to be affected by other influences at the time.

THE MOON SPEAKS

I am the Moon, here in the night sky, looking down on everything in which you mortals are involved. I am ruler of dreams, because when I am in the sky people are asleep, dreaming. I can bring them messages of events going on far away, or of things that are going to happen in the future. I am the symbol of psychics, and all those functioning on intuitive levels of awareness.

I reflect the light of the sun down to earth, and therefore am the symbol of reflection, in the sense of looking inwardly at one's own hopes, fears, dreams, and aspirations.

The path that runs between the two towers is a symbol of the need to tread "the middle way" between all extremities, as the two towers mark the gateway between the worlds of spirit and matter.

Many travelers, when they tread my way, become obsessed with the shadows they see around the edges of their field of vision. These may be actual forms of astral life which they are seeing, but very often they will just be projections of their own fears and anxieties.

In my realm it is important to recognize that what you are seeing is, in a very real sense, what you are. If something should "freak you out" on one of your journeys through my realm, the safest thing to do is to give your love to it in order to resolve the contradiction and antagonism you experience in the situation.

I also rule over the ebb and flow of all activities; when things become stronger it is because their tide has come in, and when they diminish their tide has gone out. Although I seem far away, my influence is considerable; with ease I am able to draw millions of tons of water around your world, non-stop, every day. Imagine what other more subtle, unseen influences I am able to exert, even without your noticing!

XIX The Sun

The sun hangs in the sky overlooking the Shire. Everything moves along harmoniously in this small place. The events taking place elsewhere in Middle-earth seem very distant indeed. The Shire exudes a sense of growth and harmonious development in all aspects of life.

The Shire was the homeland of Hobbits, an area of about 18,000 square miles in Eriador between the Baranduin and the Far Downs. The Shire did experience the domination of Saruman and Lotho Sackville-Baggins, and evil Men during the War of the Ring. Other than this, though, the Hobbits managed to ignore the rest of the world for so long that they almost forgot it existed. The Hobbits didn't travel much, so the Shire was little known to the rest of Middle-earth.

The social structure of the Shire was quite simple, consisting of a small landed gentry presiding over a larger group of trades-people, with a class of agricultural workers underneath them. They needed no formal government; it was a peaceful agricultural society, very likely based on an idealized vision of rural England. It is worth noting that no Hobbit ever killed another Hobbit in the Shire.

On the left, a road sign points the way into this place. Further ahead are some of the Hobbit houses, cut into the side of the hills for maximum protection against the weather, while at the same time getting maximum sunlight through their circular windows. Further on, clothes dry on a Hobbit's washing-line, and fences roll off the side of the hills as they curve into the distance. All is a picture of gentle activity and tranquillity.

TAROT MEANING

The card represents success and prosperity. In some decks children are shown playing in a garden, symbolizing the joy and innocence of liberation. It shows happiness on all levels of being and consciousness. This card can epitomize happy love affairs and marriages, everything encapsulated in the phrase "the sunny side of life."

With this card, there is a sense of growth and harmonious development in all areas of life. When people do not have objectives, they become listless, depressed, and devoid of any "get up and go." The Sun card is about having goals, and about motivating oneself to accomplish them. People often say that they feel better when the weather is bright and sunny; sometimes we need to generate our own "solar power" from within ourselves to be bright and energetic even when those around us are flooded with negativity. Imagine that you have a small sun burning inside you as you go through your daily rounds. This powerful technique will give you a small "glow," which others may notice. The glow generates protection and encourages the facilitation of material objectives. To create in your mind's eye a radiance of golden light around yourself will encourage a sunnier appearance, better health, and material prosperity. Let this technique slip in to your everyday activities. Even during seemingly commonplace activities and moments, we can consciously infuse our own "sunny" spirituality.

ASTROLOGICAL ASSOCIATION

The sun.

The sun is, by tradition, the single most important celestial body in astrology. What it shows is the basic personality, the inner essence of the person. The other planets are then taken to represent other aspects of the personality. The sun shines equally on all lands, but the influence it has depends on the countryside's ability to receive. In the land of Mordor, for instance, the dark clouds of pollution emanating from Mount Doom and the industrial and military activities of Sauron made any penetration of the sun's positive rays impossible. It can be the same with our lives. The sun is a symbol of divine blessing—it is available to as many as wish to receive it; but only those who are really open to its influence, and the benefit it can bring, will stand to benefit in reality.

The solar plexus of the human body is an energy-center which actually processes the power of the sun into a more subtle energy which the human body can then utilize. Our sun is associated with good health—and a little of its influence can go a long way toward dispelling colds and the effects of the damp.

But exposure to too much of its power can result in sunburn and even skin cancer.

THE SUN SPEAKS

Here at the top of the sky, I am shown in your astrological charts as the ruler of all the other planets, and in your own physical solar system right at the center of your universe! That is why I have always represented the rulers of your people. From me you gain the light and warmth which sustains your lives; without my continual influence you would all wither and die! I have been worshipped as a god since early times, either as a supreme deity or as an image of the godhead. Myths involving floods recall horrifying periods when I refused to shine. Solar eclipses have long been regarded with awe and fear. All over the world and throughout time, misguided humans engage in prayer, propitiation, or even human sacrifices to encourage me to shine.

At an eclipse, the Senci Indians of Peru would shoot fire arrows into the air to rekindle the light. In Norse myth my light would be dimmed for three years before the beginning of Ragnarök, the end of the world. In ancient Egypt, the Pharaoh, as a living symbol of me in my guise as Ra, would walk around the temple walls to ensure my daily journey round the sky. Brahmans still claim that without their morning offering I cannot rise, and the Aztecs annually sacrificed thousands of people to me in my aspect of Huitzilopochtli, in order to keep me moving through the sky.

My solar imagery is seen in the legends of Adonis and Tammuz, gods representing my powers to some extent, who are killed and then rise again. In the account of Christ we have a retelling of that story, for He dies and then rises again, as I do every night and every morning.

My symbols are numerous, and include a disc, an eagle, a spider sitting at the center of its web, a swastika, a revolving wheel, a lion, a ram, and a winged Chinese dragon. In the Qabalistic Tree of Life, my place is the heart center, where I preside over Tiphareth. This placement shows the union of the lower with the higher worlds.

XX Judgment

This same scene occurs for two different Hobbits—Frodo and Bilbo. This card is about choosing the direction of one's destiny. It is the axis on which "make or break" decisions are made. The fates are watching! Judgment signifies rebirth, but a different kind of rebirth from Death. It is a slow realization that one's decision could ensure the hand of fate with you or against you. For Bilbo, it was a moment of sacrifice—something he had carried too long which was no longer necessary—and also a moment of growing and taking responsibility for Frodo as keeper of the Ring.

This card portrays the encounter between Frodo and Gandalf, in which Frodo must make a vital decision. He is under extreme pressure, another aspect of the Judgment card. In the first encounter, Gandalf had refused to take the Ring from Bilbo;

however, when Bilbo dropped the envelope containing the Ring, Gandalf picked it up and placed it on the mantelpiece for him. In this scene, Gandalf does take the Ring from Frodo and throws it into the fire to show him the hidden writing upon it. This act initially shocked Frodo: thus this card also shows the effect of shocks occurring in our lives—when the totally unexpected happens and disturbs the peaceful pattern of our lives. Shock is a strange phenomenon. We all deal with it in different ways. Some of us try to minimize a shock, while others may dramatize it.

On the mantelpiece we see pipes (air), two candlesticks (fire), a clock, and a small casket containing valuables (earth). Beneath the mantelpiece we see a kettle brewing, representing water, the fourth element. Gandalf holds the One Ring in his hand.

TAROT MEANING
Powerful transformative energies; possibly emigration.

The powerful transformative energies at work are being unleashed by the Ring itself, stimulating not only its holder but all others around it to make changes in their lives which they will never be able to undo. All the decisions which the Ring forced on people were irrevocable, for good or for bad. It would bring out either the very worst or the very best in a person, with little in between. If the personality had a flaw, or a pride, or an egotism of any kind, the Ring would pick up on that and magnify it a thousand times, turning the person into an extremity of that one single characteristic. Only the strongest personalities could resist the lure of the Ring. Galadriel was tempted to become a great queen, beautiful and terrible; but she resisted the Ring. Gollum desired to be invisible, to learn secrets, to hide; and he gave in to the Ring.

Judgment was traditionally shown as three people coming out from the ground, in accordance with the literal interpretation of the Biblical prophecy that "the dead would rise bodily from the ground" upon the sounding of the trumpet by the archangel Michael. The dead would then be judged according to their faith and their actions.

Similarly, each character's reaction to what the Ring represented defined their role in the story and in their lifetime. Here, everyone is going to be judged by their faith (i.e., belief in themselves, what values they hold dear) and their actions in terms of what they do to help their own side win.

At the very center of the picture, flames transform solid fuel back into pure energy (fire). This shows the movement of one energy form into another, but never its loss from the universe.

ASTROLOGICAL ASSOCIATION
Pluto, the planet of transformation.

Pluto changes everything from one form into a completely different form, always irrevocably. After experiencing its influence, there is no way of returning back to the way things were before. Pluto also has a connection with mass movements, and the power of individuals to mobilize large numbers of people in the cause of mass movements. In the War of the Rings, for example, entire nations are raised against each other in a desperate struggle for survival and, in the case of the Orcs, for hegemony.

JUDGMENT SPEAKS
Here you are, Middle-earthlings, with your first opportunity for real transformation, and what are you going to do? Are you going to let this chance slip by, and stay in your cozy yet boring

rut? Or are you going to take up the challenge and strike out afresh? I can see all your uncertainties coming to the surface even as I speak. But I can also see all the desires for something different to occur within your life. It is this spirit to which I appeal now.

One of my symbols is the volcano, which builds up over a period of time and then finally explodes in a massive release of debris and lava. This is what will be happening in your world unless you are able to find ways of releasing and resolving some of your contradictions.

My negative aspects? Obsessive and power-controlling relationships. Sauron certainly embodies a hunger for power in *The Lord of the Rings*. This is also shown today, on an extreme level, in the growth of religious and quasi-religious cults that induce their members to give up personal responsibility and allow others to control their thoughts and actions. In times of great uncertainty, some people will find it easier to submerge their individuality in a group or movement which gives them a sense of security. Others will seek instead to get more in touch with their individuality and reassert their own life directions. There will always be a contradiction between these two, and my influence will always be to exacerbate the gulf between them.

As your society transforms, you will see many different communities, splitting off and going about doing their own thing. They will be setting up their own economic foundations, developing their own way of self-governing. It will be a kind of tribalism, and many of these groups will make mistakes—otherwise they will never learn.

XXI The World

The map of Arda shows two continents. Middle-earth is on the right. The land to the left represents the Undying Lands, which lay to the west when the world was flat; or the eastern continent, which was pulled into this position when the Undying Lands were removed from the world, and the world contracted and became round. On either side are the two pillars, reminding us of the two Lamps of the Valar and also the Two Trees.

The floor is represented as a series of seven lines of white light, converging diagonally, overlaid on a background of black, reminding us of the inevitable victory of Light over Darkness.

The scroll, as it unfolds before us, reads:

The Road goes ever on and on
Down from the door where it began.
Now far ahead the Road has gone,
And I must follow, if I can,
Pursuing it with eager feet,
Until it joins some larger way
Where many paths and errands meet.
And whither then? I cannot say.

The Road goes ever on and on...

It is the song of both Frodo and Bilbo, as they set out on their quests; and it can be the song of each of us as we set out upon our life's journeys here in this realm.

Above the pillars is a pediment with the One Ring framed within the inscription "Rings—The Lord of the Rings."

In looking at the map of Arda in this way, it is almost as though we are being invited to enter a temple of experience, which in a way we do when we incarnate on earth and are born as mortals.

TAROT MEANING

This card shows success and attainment. It represents bringing everything together so that it stands on its own and taking responsibility for one's actions.

The earth is inhabited by a spirit that is its life and soul. Some of the names by which the Earth Mother is known include Danu, Gaia, Lakshmi. The Earth Mother is not always kind: mines collapse, volcanoes erupt, earthquakes occur. Some think that patriarchal religions drew us away from a deep respect of the Earth Mother, insisting that Adam created Eve, not vice versa, denying natural cycles and the older wisdom as a fairy tale. Whatever could not be weighed and measured has been rejected over the centuries. The process by which this happened was gradual. Christian conquistadors rededicated the holy sites of the people they slew, while Protestants in North America scorned Earth Mother notions as pagan. Some people throughout the world today still recognize that energy flows through the earth, forming dragon paths, or ley-lines, and seems to follow seasonal magnetic currents. The properties of streams, rivers, and lakes follow similar patterns. Sacred sites which contain a particular essence of the Earth Mother have been converted into religious sites in some places, in other instances they are held to be centers of paganism, or "the old religion."

The earth lives, not in any anthropomorphic sense, but as a complex and living organism. It is unwise for us to ignore the Earth Mother: she is the life force which sustains us, clothes us in our physical bodies with our senses, and gives us our health. When she is hard on us, through natural calamity, we recognize her power and begin to respect her, awed at the damage done. Unless we as a race can begin to change our ways and avoid destroying the environment, she will pursue us, and eventually see that we experience the fruits of destruction from the seeds that we have planted.

Mysterious Neolithic earth mounds are found all over the world—there are some 40,000 in Britain alone. The myths connected with these mounds usually involve giants, "barrow-wights," ghosts, and dragons who guard buried treasure. There are some long barrows (over 300 feet long) which are said to contain the bodies of giants. Yet not all had the primary purpose of burial; they were probably placed there to increase the land's fertility. In Ireland, at New Grange, the main stone passageway is carved with spirals, and becomes charged with power at midwinter sunrise. In Ohio, the great serpent mound snakes over hundreds of yards, and is one of many animal mounds invoking fertility symbolism through sun and serpent. In China, and now increasingly here in the west, Feng Shui is practiced to align earth energies and bring about a greater sense of harmony for the home and productivity for the workplace.

The symbol of earthly paradise which lies to the west, epitomized in Tolkien's Undying Lands, is an ancient one. This is found in many traditions; it is always a land which only heroes and heroines are able to enter, where they enjoy eternal youth, fountains, and beautiful gardens. In the Christian tradition it was heaven, a garden of Eden brought back full circle. In Buddhism it was the state of enlightenment resulting from meditation. The concept of earthly paradise was different from the heavenly state of these two faiths in that it always lay to the west. This idea still persists in modern idiom in the expression, "Go west, young man."

Negative aspects of this card include carrying the world upon your shoulders; having excessive duties and heavy responsibilities; and dealing with issues that leave you uncertain, depressed, or lonesome. Experiences with teachers, older people, or guide figures might be indicated by this card.

ASTROLOGICAL ASSOCIATION

Saturn, the planet symbolic of building, creating, and making things real and lasting.

Saturn is also the planet of challenges from the material, real world, making us get our act together to be able to achieve the things that are important to us. Under such conditions, it can create a sense of isolation, even despondency, in the lives of those who experience it. It is therefore aligned in its negative aspect with depression, a world-weariness, and a sense of carrying heavy burdens and excessive responsibilities in life.

In Roman mythology, Saturn was an ancient corn god identified with Chronos, and he ruled Italy during the Golden Age until Jupiter drove him from the sky. The prosperity he brought is still celebrated in the feast of Saturnalia, from the 17th to the 23rd of December.

The metal associated with Saturn is lead, and some have suggested that the domestic use of this metal in Rome created lead poisoning over the centuries, which led to the decline of the Roman spirit. The symptoms include sluggishness, gloominess, and a general lack of enthusiasm.

THE WORLD SPEAKS

I am Arda, the sphere in which you live and experience everything possible while you are here in your physical form. I have given you substance, and unto me you will render your bodies when you have worn them out with the experience of your lives.

It is through my co-operation that you become able to put anything together that is tangible and lasting so that others can appreciate your inspiration and initiative. I am a hard taskmaster. I insist on attention to detail; if something is left undone, the chances are that I will find it and expose it.

All your fancy schemes of positive thinking eventually come under my laws, so don't put all of your eggs into any one basket. When your expectation meets reality, you had better have all your hatches battened down. I won't be there to give you any second chances. Preparation is the key note for any successful endeavor. I have much to do with the foundations which you establish for yourselves when you begin any undertaking. The foundations must be level, securely laid, and stable before any superstructure can be placed upon them. The same principles must apply to your activities in a metaphoric sense. That is why honesty, fairness, and integrity are so important to me: nothing can last without these qualities.

IV
The Minor Arcana

THE SUIT OF SWORDS

Swords relate to states of mind and situations of conflict. Conflict is not always bad; sometimes it is necessary to clear the air and to forestall wrongdoing and negativity. Without confronting and exposing evil, the good influences would not have a chance to grow and develop. Without the Rangers' protection, the Hobbits would have had a tougher time long before the War of the Ring ever started. One of the most prominent symbols of *The Lord of the Rings* is the sword, which ruthlessly cut down the enemies of good and re-established the sanctity of the kingdom against invading peoples or influences. The sword also symbolizes the ability of the intellect to cut through problems.

In mythology, the sword represents power, authority, and the masculine principle. It is the phallus; and the sheath in which it is kept is the receptive feminine principle. The hero's sword imparts tremendous powers, and is an indicator of his masculinity. In hero-myth the sword is very often given to the mortal by the gods, after a test to prove he is worthy of using it. Arthur is the only one who can draw out the sword Excalibur from the stone to establish himself as the true king of England. In Norse myth, Sigmund is the only one who can pull the sword Balmung from the tree into which Odin has thrust it. Later on in the story, Siegfried is the only one who can forge the sword that has been broken, after the Dwarf Mime has tried and failed countless times. (There is a tendency for swords to have their own names, which anthropomorphizes them.)

ACE OF SWORDS

Gwaihir, Lord of the Eagles of the Misty Mountains, befriended Gandalf after the wizard healed the eagle's poisoned wound. The eagles participated in the Battle of the Five Armies, and their intervention played a crucial role. Later, Gwaihir helped Gandalf three times: he freed Gandalf from Saruman's tower after his imprisonment there; then freed Gandalf from the peak of Zirak-zigil after his battle with the Balrog; and finally, Gwaihir rescued Frodo and Sam from Mount Doom, after the Ring had been cast into the fire. This great bird—and his fellows—served Gandalf and Radagast the Brown as messengers and as spies, letting them know what was going on in the countryside. Above him, written in runes, are the words, "Lord of the Misty Mountains: Gwaihir."

Tarot Meaning
A liberating situation or opportunity that enables rapid progress to be made now. Breakthrough.

TWO OF SWORDS

The table of the Council of Elrond displays the names of the Nine chosen by Elrond to return the One Ring to the fires of Mount Doom. In the center of the table is the One Ring and Aragorn's broken sword, which has come to him through 39 generations from Isildur, signifying his right to rule in Gondor. A ray of light, showing spiritual illumination, descends, forming a triangle on the table as this force materializes. The ten spokes of the wheel show the different symbols of the participants: the leaf for Elrond, the sword hilt for Aragorn, the musical note for Pippin, the fire for Gandalf, the Ring for Frodo, the branch for Sam, the ax for Gimli, the arrow for Legolas, the horn for Boromir, and the red flower for Merry. Underneath the table is the runic "G," the symbol of Gandalf, who is the real support behind this assortment of different forces.

Tarot Meaning
Indecision. Coming to grips with a problem.

THREE OF SWORDS

Sam comforts Frodo after the Ring is destroyed in the Cracks of Doom. Frodo was unable to cast the Ring into the fire, and it was only through the unexpected intervention of Gollum—who attacked Frodo, bit off his finger with the Ring, and fell backwards into the fire—that the Ring was destroyed. In the background we see Gwaihir flying through the air to come and pick them both up. They are as yet unaware of the full implications of the destruction of the Ring; already the Black Riders have disintegrated, and the Orc armies of Mordor are fleeing in disarray. It is a scene of apparent heartbreak, but it contains the seeds of tremendous victory.

Tarot Meaning
Heartbreak, but as a precursor to greater victory and success than can currently be imagined. The need for much more communication, rather than less, in order to break through the misunderstandings and contradictions of the present.

FOUR OF SWORDS

Frodo is sitting by an ancient stone monument with the first blush of morning dawning over the horizon. The scene is from the morning after the attack of the Barrow-wight, and Frodo is relieved at having survived. The Barrow-wights were evil spirits who infested the Barrow-downs and lured people into the barrows, imprisoning them forever under evil spells. Burial mounds exist all over Europe, and, in the form of the Native American mounds, in the United States as well. In Europe, they have always been places of rest for ancient kings. Often caverns lay beneath these mounds, serving as a kind of crypt. (In this representation, we have been inspired by the ancient stone monument at Trethevy Quoit in Cornwall.)

Tarot Meaning
The lifting of tensions; relief at having passed some ordeal or test of one's powers.

FIVE OF SWORDS

Pippin and Merry have been captured by the Orcs, who are arguing amongst themselves about their prisoners. The White Hand symbol of Saruman and the Red Eye of Sauron are inscribed on the Orcs' shields, as the raiding party was a collaboration between these two forces. Grishnákh, with the Red Eye of Mordor on his chest, leans over the two Companions. The Orcs killed Boromir when they captured Merry and Pippin, then quarreled over the prisoners. Grishnákh tried to steal the prisoners from the White Hand Orcs when they became surrounded by the Rohirrim, but he was killed by the riders after Pippin and Merry had been taken far enough away to enable them to escape. From his conversation with the other Orcs, it is clear that Grishnákh knew something of the tension between Sauron and Saruman. He had also discovered the secret of the One Ring, and tried to get it for himself.

Tarot Meaning
Crossed swords; the parting of ways between people.

SIX OF SWORDS

From *The Hobbit:* the Dwarves and Bilbo Baggins are escaping from the Elves, floating down the river inside barrels. In the distance looms Lake-town, a town inhabited by humans, where the Dwarves and Bilbo were given food and shelter.

Tarot Meaning
Escape. Sailing away from negativity. Retreat from a situation of defeat, captivity, or limitation.

SEVEN OF SWORDS

In this scene we see two Trolls from *The Hobbit*—Bert and Bill—fighting amongst themselves. The third Troll, Tom, is not in the picture. In the story, the Trolls had succeeded in capturing the party of Dwarves, but Gandalf successfully imitated their voices and provoked a fight among them. In the bags which are lying tied up on the ground are the Dwarves who accompanied Bilbo Baggins. When the sun came up, the three Trolls were turned to stone.

Tarot Meaning
Making an important sacrifice for a long-term benefit. Taking something (or having something taken) without being entitled to it.

EIGHT OF SWORDS

Sam discovers Frodo lying bitten, paralyzed, bound in the web of Shelob. Frodo's Elven sword, which he had dropped, lies on the ground. Sam snatched up the sword, attacked Shelob, and succeeded in driving her off. He then sets about cutting Frodo free from the bonds of limitation which Shelob had spun about him. The emphasis is on seeing no escape.

Tarot Meaning
A situation of frustration. Awaiting the moment when you will be set free, but the need for some patience before that can happen.

NINE OF SWORDS

The Nine Ringwraiths (Black Riders) gather together before the climactic battle under the leadership of their Captain, the Witch-king, who sits at the center atop his steed. On either side we see the pillars of the gateway leading out from Sauron's kingdom of Mordor, while the shadowy outline of the Dark Lord is seen hovering above them. Crowning him is the Red Eye, inscribed within the triangle. The Nine were kings and powerful individuals before their enslavement by Sauron. He captured them by offering them Rings of Power, appealing to their sense of greed, aggrandizement, and desire for control. Thus, in seeking all these things, they actually lost them, and became shadowy creatures without any will or life of their own. The two eyes also represent the collective hypnotism of the Black Riders.

This card signifies being cruelly led from your path and imprisoned in a loss of will, just as the Black Riders would subdue their victims through the powers of the evil Black Breath. The swords here are curved scimitars, the preferred weapon of the Orcs.

Tarot Meaning

The feeling of having your hands tied. Difficulties in getting out of your present predicament. Isolation, alienation; overcoming these conditions through greater communication with others around you.

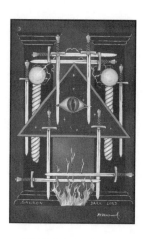

TEN OF SWORDS

We enter the abode of the Dark Lord, and see before us the Red Eye of Sauron. As we move closer, under his unblinking gaze, the swords around us become activated and begin to seal us in, preventing our escape. The Van de Graaf generators start humming, and we see and hear electricity crackling from the orbs on either side. Every now and again we see a burst of electrical discharge shoot from one sphere to the other, while at our feet a panel opens up and flames leap up. We find ourselves in the grip of Sauron!

Tarot Meaning
Big changes in life, and the need to be sufficiently flexible to go along with them. Also, extreme limitation, and the need to extricate yourself from intolerable conditions by taking responsibility and stiffening personal resolution.

PAGE OF SWORDS

Denethor, with Pippin, looks into the Palantír for signs of what the coming battle for Minas Tirith will hold. He sees signs of doom and gloom, which unbeknownst to him were inspired by Sauron. On the floor Denethor has various scrolls containing orders to his troops. Above his head we see his sword framed against the elemental symbol of air, the triangle with the horizontal bar. This triangle is part of a much greater mandala, just as Denethor's struggle is part of a much greater battle.

Tarot Meaning
The need to avoid rushing into battle. The necessity of getting all the relevant information before making any decisive or irrevocable moves.

KNIGHT OF SWORDS

A montage of scenes from the battle for Minas Tirith. Gandalf is riding Shadowfax, leading a charge of horsemen, as he did to save Faramir before the city was surrounded and in the Battle of the Pelennor Fields, in which the siege was broken. The Rohirrim and the Princes of Dol Amroth are behind him. Under the horse's hooves is a shield bearing the Red Eye of Mordor, while the battle rages around him. In the background and to the side, the Men of Harad, allies of Sauron, use the "Oliphaunts" and other means to break and scale the walls. Overhead flies one of the Nazgûl mounts. Gandalf's sword Glamdring hovers above, passing through a shield representing Gondor. This scene represents among the most important events in the story, as it swung the entire balance of power.

Tarot Meaning
Having the balance of power in one's favor; the need to solve conflict through careful thinking coupled with decisive action.

QUEEN OF SWORDS

The Lady Éowyn symbolically subjugates the Witch-king's steed before decapitating it. The Witch-king himself lies off-picture, out of sight—she will be killing him shortly, as well. Behind the steed flies the banner of the Rohirrim. In the battle for Pelennor Fields she played a very decisive role. Just as the Witch-king's battering ram Grond broke down the main gate, the Rohirrim attacked, led by Théoden and Éowyn's brother Éomer. Seeing victory about to be snatched from his grasp, the Black Captain intervened. Théoden's horse went down, crushing his rider, and the Rohirrim horses panicked as he approached.

Éowyn, disguised as a man in armor, challenged the Witch-king as he sat gloating over the bodies of King Théoden and his horse Snowmane. The Witch-king did not at first take her seriously, and reminded her of the prophecy that no living man could slay him. She replied that she was not a living man, but a woman, and as he descended upon her, Éowyn beheaded his mount's head with her sword. The Witch-king's heavy mace smashed her shield into pieces. As he raised his arm for the final blow, Merry rushed behind him and plunged his sword into the back of the Witch-king's knee, which gave Éowyn time to recover and run her blade through the Witch-king's neck.

Tarot Meaning
A determined woman who, like Éowyn, will not be swayed from her purpose.

KING OF SWORDS

Aragorn receives his crown, and now regains his throne. This is a symbolic picture, for the actual coronation took place before Arwen arrived; nor is this the actual crown. Kings have many crowns: day crowns, mourning crowns, war crowns, ceremonial crowns, etc. The crown in this picture is not a ceremonial crown. Ceremonial crowns were much too heavy to wear all the time. They were well nigh impossible to wear in battle—and far too valuable. If a king wished to be instantly recognizable to his army, he would have to wear a lesser crown over the helm. In her hands the Lady Arwen holds Aragorn's battle helmet. Aragorn has succeeded in turning the tide and saving the race of Men against Mordor. Aragorn will now marry Arwen, and go about the problems of rebuilding the kingdom from the damage done during the war.

Tarot Meaning
You have won the war; now you must win the peace.

The Suit of Wands

This suit represents the element fire, and indicates situations and conditions involving energy, action, and initiative. The harnessing of fire was probably the biggest step in the growth of human culture. In the story of Prometheus, the gods punish Prometheus for stealing fire from heaven and bringing it down to humanity. With the controlled use of fire, human beings could cook, see in the darkness, and keep wild animals at bay. In the mythology of the Vikings, the union of water and fire creates all life. In alchemy, the divine fiery water is the first outflowing of the Word of God. According to one legend, there was no material universe until Lucifer, attempting to carry out this alchemy, tried to manipulate these elements. King Nebuchadnezzar threw Shadrach, Meshach, and Abednego into the fiery furnace when they refused to worship his golden idol. They emerged without even being singed, thus demonstrating the power of Yahweh.

The element of fire has always been seen as an earthly expression of the power of the sun god, who rises each day and, although "dying" in winter, returns to life each spring (it also "dies" each night and returns every morning). The ancient fire festivals carried out by our pagan ancestors were a means of invoking this essence. Beltane, in May, represented clearing out all the dead wood of life to make room for the new growth.

In New Caledonia, the sunshine is summoned to earth by a shaman who climbs to the top of a mountain with a collection of magical charms and sets fire to the bundle as the sun rises from the sea. When floods threaten, the aboriginals in Australia throw fire sticks into the air in order to drive away rain. In India, widowed wives were pressed into throwing themselves onto the funeral pyres of their deceased husbands; the British Raj outlawed this practice. All across the world, the use of fire to dispose of the dead is commonplace (although not in such an extreme form as this), symbolizing the return to the Earth Mother.

Fire has often been used to symbolize the presence of the deity. When Moses met God, the latter appeared in the form of the burning bush. The appearance of "tongues of flame" over the heads of the apostles represented the presence and inspiration of the holy spirit. In ancient Rome the hearth was sacred to the goddess Vesta (she even has a brand of matches named after her in Britain called Swan Vestas). In Native American culture, the fire at the center of the Medicine Lodge is the symbolic home of the Great Spirit.

In Norse mythology the fire-god archetype was represented by Thor, who was also a blacksmith god. Other pantheons had a similar image, such as the Greek god Hephaestus (Vulcan), who forged the thunderbolts of Zeus and the weapons of the other gods deep in the center of the earth, underneath volcanoes. Fire was also worshipped as a symbol of divinity by the Zoroastrians in Persia, and as Marduk in Babylon and Kali in India.

Fire is also closely associated with Thoth Tehuti of the ancient Egyptians, Hermes of the Greeks, and Mercury of the Romans: all these different aspects of the "god of knowledge" are linked with realization and consciousness. The Mayan fire god Heuheutlotl is shown in stone statues with a fire brazier on his head, while the Hawaiian volcano goddess Pele was always prone to burning to death anyone she didn't like. Tolkien refers to the "Flame Imperishable" and the "Secret Fire," which seem to represent the soul, the "spark of life" of a conscious Being which comes only from Ilúvatar (God).

Wands have always been an attribute of magicians, as the symbolic lightning rod which brings down the power of the gods onto earth. Moses was able to perform miracles through the use of his wand, which, when he threw it onto the floor, became a serpent that ate up the transformed wands of Pharaoh's magicians. In fairy lore, wands granted divine insight into other dimensions. The wand of Hypnos granted forgetfulness and sleep, hence the derivation of his name in "hypnotism." The wand was also used by Joseph of Arimathea for support, and when he arrives at Glastonbury it begins to sprout into a tree, thus indicating to him that this was where God wanted him to remain and set up the world's first Christian church. In Middle-earth, the Istari (wizards) bear magical staffs; and when Gandalf the White deposes Saruman, Saruman's staff breaks.

ACE OF WANDS

The volcano Mount Doom (Orodruin), on the plain of Gorgoroth, in Mordor, where in the Second Age Sauron forged the One Ring in order to gain control over the other Rings of Power. The volcano was only about 4,500 feet high, but because it stood alone seemed much taller than it was. Entering through a hole bored into the side, one came to the Cracks of Doom, in the bottom of which burned the Fire of Doom. The forge on which Sauron made the Ring is in the front, inscribed within a circle, showing infinity, and a square, representing manifestation. On the top of the square is the runic symbol for north; to the right, east; at the bottom, south; and finally to the left, the symbol for west. On the side of the anvil is the upward-pointing triangle, signifying fire.

Tarot Meaning
New enterprise; individual initiative.

TWO OF WANDS

Gandalf leans on his staff, looking east toward the land of Mordor. In the distance lie the towers of Barad-dûr, Sauron's Dark Tower, with the single unblinking Red Eye of Sauron overhead, looking for him.

Tarot Meaning
Good advice, given and received.

THREE OF WANDS

Aragorn, Legolas, and Gimli are attempting to rescue Pippin and Merry, who have been captured by the Orc raiders. Aragorn has seen a sign on the ground, the small leaf-shaped Elven brooch dropped by Pippin. He points to it while resting for a moment on the shoulder of Gimli. Behind them is the outline of a stone circle.

Tarot Meaning
Leading others by example; loyalty toward one's friends/group.

FOUR OF WANDS

In the Hall of Théoden, Gandalf talks to the king, showing him the wisdom of preparing for a confrontation against Saruman in what little time is left. In front of him kneels Éomer, his nephew, with whom Théoden is now reconciled.

Tarot Meaning
Working with other people in a spirit of reconciliation and co-operation toward a common goal.

FIVE OF WANDS

A scene from *The Hobbit*. Bilbo Baggins passes through Mirkwood. The great spiders there were all descendants of Shelob, and had infested the forest where they would capture Men, Hobbits, and whoever else they could, spinning them into their webs to eat later on. After the War of the Ring, this place was cleansed of these invidious creatures and renamed Eryn Lasgalen ("green wood"). In this representation, the Dwarves are still bound and spiders are present. It is up to Bilbo to save them. Bilbo's race against time is being thwarted by the forces of negativity.

Tarot Meaning
There is strong competition, but work assiduously against your opposition.

SIX OF WANDS

We see here the Battle of the Five Armies from *The Hobbit*, with Beorn in the center and Gwaihir overhead leading the Army of Eagles. Beorn was a shape-changer, a huge man who could turn into a bear; in the Battle, he fought as a bear. On the side of humanity were the Dwarves of Erebor and the Elves of Northern Mirkwood. Against them were united a vast army of Orcs and wolves of the Misty Mountains. The Men were led by Bard, the Elves by Thranduil, and the Dwarves by Thorin Oakenshield and Dain Ironfoot.

Tarot Meaning
Victory against the forces of negativity. Take time out to take a bow.

SEVEN OF WANDS

Aragorn reaches to pick up a burning branch from the fire. He encouraged Pippin, Frodo, and Merry (not shown here) to do the same in order to fend off the attack of the Black Riders, who were searching for them on Weathertop. Fire was an effective way of resisting the Black Riders, and Aragorn used it to good advantage in this situation. The Riders (Ringwraiths) are not visible, being outside the picture.

Tarot Meaning
Cut down your problems one by one. Don't let them build up and overwhelm you.

EIGHT OF WANDS

Gandalf rides Shadowfax at great speed. Shadowfax was the fastest horse in Middle-earth, descendant of the Mearas, the royal horses of Rohan. He would permit none but Gandalf to ride him. Gandalf needs to get from one place to another very quickly in order to achieve his objectives. He does not wear his hat, as it would be likely to fall off at such a speed!

Tarot Meaning
One's life is speeding up; things are happening quickly. Messages coming in and going out.

NINE OF WANDS

In this situation, Gandalf is in disagreement with Saruman the White, who has transformed himself into Saruman of Many Colors. Saruman sits on the left, while Gandalf the Grey is on the right. Saruman has attempted to persuade Gandalf to reveal the location of the Ring. He has tried to appeal to Gandalf's desire for power, even to his sense of history. But Gandalf has heard this all before and will not be swayed from his dedication.

Tarot Meaning
Taking down your barriers once genuine trust has been firmly established.

TEN OF WANDS

Sam carries Frodo on the final leg of the journey to Mount Doom. Frodo has lost the strength to move himself, so great has the weight of the Ring become upon him, both physically and spiritually.

Tarot Meaning
Carrying the burdens of others: but don't let it become a habit.

PAGE OF WANDS

Radagast the Brown, one of the five Istari (wizards), personifies the spirit of nature and is knowledgeable about herbs and animals. He has a special bond with birds, and played a more indirect role in the War of the Ring. He is a messenger, and is shown carrying a staff. He may convey messages through his telepathic powers. Radagast the Brown unwittingly caused Gandalf to be captured by Saruman, for Saruman had deceived Radagast with a message for Gandalf; but Radagast also enabled Gandalf to escape, by dispatching Gwaihir to Gandalf with news.

Tarot Meaning
Learning and/or traveling. A message of importance coming to you from someone afar.

KNIGHT OF WANDS

This picture shows Faramir walking alongside a small stream, his bow and arrows at hand in case he should unexpectedly come across a party of Orcs. Faramir was the second son of Denethor, and was a gentle personality who did not enjoy fighting for its own sake, but who nonetheless battled with great courage. He was popular with his own troops, although his own father was closer to Boromir, his older brother. He was injured by an arrow and by the Black Breath of the Ringwraiths during the siege of Minas Tirith, and while he was recovering he met and fell in love with Éowyn. They were married, and Faramir became Steward of Gondor after the end of the War.

Tarot Meaning
Dynamic male energy.

QUEEN OF WANDS

The woman shown here is Théodwyn, beloved sister of King Théoden of Rohan, who married Éomund of Eastfold and bore him two children, Éomer and Éowyn. Both Théodwyn and her husband died young, and her children were raised in the household of Théoden. They distinguished themselves in the War of the Ring: Éomer at Helm's Deep, Pelennor Fields, and Morannon; Éowyn by slaying the Witch-king before the gates of Minas Tirith. After the death of Théodred, his only son, King Théoden named Éomer his successor. On Théodwyn's lap is an arrow (emblem of Sagittarius) and the outline of a lion's mane (Leo), both symbols linking her with fire.

Tarot Meaning
An independent-minded woman who intends to exert her influence, either directly or indirectly, on the situation as it develops.

KING OF WANDS

King Théoden is with Gríma Wormtongue, who gives delete-rious advice to the king and generally undermines his confidence. The king is deep in doubt, and by his troubled brow it is clear that he is not happy with the decision Worm-tongue is manipulating him into making. Théoden has dropped the wand of authority. After Wormtongue has been exposed and his influence eliminated, Théoden will pick up the wand again, symbolically, and lead his people against Saruman.

Tarot Meaning
A man of leadership who inspires others to confidence in themselves and their future.

THE SUIT OF CUPS

This suit represents emotions and feelings, and the element water. In this modern age it is not easy for us to imagine the reverence with which the ancients regarded water. All we have to do is turn a tap, and there it is, in as great a supply as we could wish. When we experience drought, though, we are suddenly reminded how fragile our lives are without this most essential element.

As the ocean, this element has always been imagined as timeless, without beginning or end, and has been considered the source of all life. Human civilization arose by the side of rivers: the Tigris and Euphrates, the Nile, and the Yellow River in China. In Sumerian legends, Apsu, the sweet waters, and Ansu, the bitter, were the source of Tiamat, the ferocious Mother of all Creation. Tiamat was later killed by Marduk, who then split her body into the different parts of the physical universe.

Water also has a magical aspect. In legends and folklore, water was known to cure illness, resuscitate the dead, and to purify. In ancient Mosaic law one's sins could be eradicated by numerous washings and bodily purifications.

Water is an important symbol in the Bible. Jesus turned water into wine, thus showing the end of the period of the ceremonial Mosaic law. In Greek mythology, Dionysus does the same thing, although the symbolism here is based more on the principle of revelry. Most of the great visions of the prophets are by the side of water; for instance, Ezekiel's vision of the Wheels by the side of the River Jordan, and John's vision of Revelation by the cliffside on the island of Patmos where he was imprisoned and eventually died. Passage through water is also very profound, as it signifies rebirth: the Nile is turned into blood by Moses, who later parts the Red Sea, and Joshua leads his people through the

River Jordan into the Promised Land. Jesus is baptized by John the Baptist in the River Jordan, and describes himself as "the Water of Life," emphasizing that "He who drinks of me shall not thirst." The four great rivers of Genesis flow in the four cardinal directions from the Garden of Eden, nourishing the world. In Hinduism they flow from underneath Mount Meru, abode of Lord Shiva.

Wells, lakes, and rivers are held in folklore to contain various mystical properties. Often they are the home of dragons or gods or goddesses, including the Lady of the Lake, Cerridwen, mermaids, sirens, and water nymphs. Throughout the world, great serpents are spotted in lakes and the sea: Nessie in Loch Ness, for example. In Indian myth, the Nagas, a race of shape-changing serpent-people, were said to live at the bottom of the sea. In modern day superstition, we still throw coins into wishing wells, perhaps echoing an ancient practice of making an offering to the water spirits.

Water is the opposite of fire. These two elements are the conflicting opposites which ultimately merge together. Just as water is of the Earth Mother, so fire is of the Sky Father. At different periods the world is said to be destroyed by fire (the fall of Atlantis, Mu, and Lemuria), and at others the destroyer is water (Noah, Manu).

Fortune-tellers, or "diviners," use water to pick up and magnify psychic impressions. The symbol of the Vescia Pisces shows two streams merging together, and is a symbol of the two underground streams in Glastonbury, under the Tor and Chalice Hill (the masculine and feminine energies, respectively). Megalithic stone circles are sometimes placed over the crossing of two streams such as this.

The use of the cup or chalice reminds us of the Holy Grail, the relic which was used in the Last Supper, or the vessel which caught Christ's blood, brought by Joseph of Arimathea to Glastonbury. It is said to be buried underneath Chalice Hill, from which issues a red, blood-like water, which is rich in iron and, curiously, slightly radioactive. Some claim that the Grail was the Ark of the Covenant, now said to be held in the city of Axum in Ethiopia. The Grail also has antecedents in the Celtic cauldron of plenty.

ACE OF CUPS

Galadriel leads Frodo and Sam into her garden to look into her Mirror. The Mirror was a silver basin, filled with water from the stream; when Galadriel breathed upon the Mirror it would show images, scenes both commanded and unasked for. Some were scenes which had happened, but others were only visions of what might be, making it dangerous as a guide for action. The Ring Nenya shines from Galadriel's hand, capturing the energy of the stars and refracting it outward. In this picture she is warning Frodo not to touch the water, as he has just come close to doing so.

Tarot Meaning
Emotional fulfillment, or a vision of how that may be attained.

TWO OF CUPS

The War of the Ring ends, and Faramir and Éowyn embrace, having found in each other the complementary part of their own personalities. In the courtyard, Aragorn has replanted the white seedling and the White Tree of Gondor is growing again. Above, the skies are radiant. The two birds in the sky are reminiscent of the eagle that brought tidings of the Fall of Sauron as Faramir and Éowyn embraced on the parapet.

Tarot Meaning
A new relationship, or a new stage in an existing relationship.

THREE OF CUPS

Frodo rejoins Bilbo Baggins at his residence in Rivendell. Along the spines of the books on his shelf we see the word "Westmarch," which is the historical account of Middle-earth that so engrossed Bilbo. On the cover of the book he is holding is an "Om" sign, hinting at the value of meditation in our lives. Frodo is recounting his adventures to Bilbo, who will record them.

Tarot Meaning
Reunion with old friends. The celebration of rediscovering someone from the past.

FOUR OF CUPS

A symbolic scene: Frodo and Sam, here joined with Pippin and Merry, are just starting out on their journey together.

Tarot Meaning
Reaching out for new friendships.

FIVE OF CUPS

The Companions of the Fellowship have come through the Mines of Moria. But Gandalf, their guide, has fallen into the abyss in the fight with the Balrog, and now they must make it on their own. Boromir stands with his horn, Aragorn with his sword, and Legolas with his bow. To the right we see Gimli, bearing his ax, while Pippin and Merry sit before Aragorn. Frodo sits with his hood over his head, trying to decide what to do. All are grieving for Gandalf.

Tarot Meaning
Sadness, resulting from a deep emotional loss. The need to be courageous and self-reliant.

SIX OF CUPS

Pippin and Merry rest after the destruction of Isengard by the Ents, smoking the pipeweed they found in Saruman's stock. Saruman is inside, guarded from escaping by the Ents. Soon Gandalf and the others will arrive.

Tarot Meaning
Rediscovering the "child within," a sense of the basic playfulness in life. Giving and receiving on an emotional level.

SEVEN OF CUPS

This card shows the seven Palantíri, and is an extremely important card in this deck. The Palantíri were crystal globes wrought long ago by Fëanor, the greatest of the Elven-smiths, and brought to Middle-earth by Elendil after fleeing the destruction of Númenor. They showed things far away in time and space. One was placed in each of the major cities in Middle-earth. Three were lost in war. Sauron gained the stone of Minas Ithil when his Ringwraiths conquered that city. Through it, Sauron was able to warp the minds of Saruman and Denethor. Wormtongue threw the Palantír of Orthanc at Saruman (and Gandalf); Gandalf gave it to Aragorn. As heir of Isildur, Elendil's son, Aragorn had the right to use it. By looking into the Palantír, Aragorn was able to see the approaching fleet of Corsairs, as well as many other things. After the War of the Ring, Aragorn used his stone to see the condition of his kingdom.

The Palantíri were connected to each other by energy. A person of strong will could learn to control their energy by possessing one sphere. When Sauron captured the stone of Minas Ithil, the others became too dangerous to use. The other main spheres were used by Saruman and Denethor. In this picture we see the line of the three main spheres. Imagine Sauron at the center controlling the other two; he would have all three and would therefore end up controlling all seven. It is possible to visualize many aspects, magically.

When Isengard fell, Aragorn broke the spell and took control of one of the spheres, which changed the course of Sauron and gave victory to the West.

Tarot Meaning
Confusion; the need to get a clearer perspective before making a major decision. Getting one's priorities in order.

EIGHT OF CUPS

Gollum is leading Frodo and Sam through the Dead Marshes toward Mordor. There had been a great battle here once, between Men and Elves and Orcs, and the marshes covered the graves. But dead faces could still be seen under the water, and ghostly lights flickered about. Sam is looking down at the faces, and Gollum is telling him not to. The spirits of the dead ignited "tricksy" corpse-candles, which could lure travelers to their doom in the marsh.

Tarot Meaning
Looking for something on a deeper level than can be immediately found; the need to continue one's quest.

NINE OF CUPS

This card shows the celebration in the Shire at Bilbo Baggins' Eleventy-first Birthday Party. At this party he intended to disappear, leaving his home, wealth, and Ring to Frodo his nephew, whose 33rd birthday fell on the same day (September 22). All the other Hobbits are around the table, with Gandalf's fireworks in the background, and the string of lanterns hung on a line in the dusk. Frodo holds out his cup, and extends his middle finger, almost as if to signify assent of the mission that fate is about to bestow upon him.

Tarot Meaning
Experience life as a celebration.

TEN OF CUPS

Into the horizon sails the ship carrying Elrond, Galadriel, Gandalf, Bilbo, and Frodo. On the quay side we see Círdan, one of the wisest of the Sindarin Elves. He was a master mariner and shipwright. He was the owner of Narya, the Ring of Fire, until he gave it to Gandalf. He was also a member of the White Council, and fought against Sauron. Círdan will remain in Middle-earth, serving with his wisdom and his ships, until the last Elven ship sails.

Tarot Meaning
Emotional commitments and responsibilities fulfilled; or, a look at how they may be fulfilled.

PAGE OF CUPS

The scene is set in the Prancing Pony Inn, where the innkeeper Barliman Butterbur draws a tankard of frothing ale. On the left is the miserable form of Bill Ferny, the cruel keeper of Bill the Pony and later an agent of Saruman. Strider (Aragorn) rests in an armchair, smoking his pipe.

Tarot Meaning
New social or professional contacts.

KNIGHT OF CUPS

Frodo sits on Asfaloth, Glorfindel's horse, which has just carried him across the Ford of Loudwater (Bruinen) toward Rivendell. Frodo has crossed the water, and will turn to face his persecutors in an act of defiance. He suffers a grievous wound from the Morgul blade. The great flood of water created by Elrond rushes past him, sweeping away the Black Riders (Ringwraiths), with the images of white horses added by Gandalf.

Tarot Meaning
An emotionally sensitive and aware man. A situation in which one's loyalties and commitments are put to the test.

QUEEN OF CUPS

Goldberry, wife of Tom Bombadil, walks through the forest. She was a water spirit, and daughter of the River-woman of Withywindle. She was somewhat Elf-like, golden-haired and beautiful, calm, with qualities of love and compassion. The butterfly, symbol of transformation, reminds us that love can change its form, while the dragonfly represents the fascination of all creatures with the light. Goldberry personifies an aspect of the river.

Tarot Meaning
An emotionally sensitive woman who embodies the qualities of love and compassion.

KING OF CUPS

The card depicts Thorin Oakenshield and Gimli son of Glóin. Thorin led the Dwarf expedition to recover his ancestral treasure from the dragon Smaug, in Erebor the Lonely Mountain, east of Mirkwood. Gimli was one of the Nine Companions of the Ring, who, after the War of the Ring, went to the Glittering Caves in Rohan and founded a Dwarf colony there. Gimli's father Glóin was one of Thorin's companions. The river of time flows between Gimli and Thorin Oakenshield. The counsel is to await your time, for time heals all.

Tarot Meaning
An emotionally sensitive man, capable of both giving and receiving love.

THE SUIT OF COINS

The suit of coins represents the element earth, and shows material, financial, economic, and work aspects. It relates to the things which we own, the commitments we enter into, our obligations and responsibilities. This suit encourages us to consider our duties, how we control our space, what we do with our time, and how we deal with the limitations pertaining to each of these spheres.

The spiral is used to illustrate the coins. Spirals are often found in nature: sea shells, snail shells, the ear, animal horns, the coiled serpent. We see the spiral in a more universal context in the movements of the planets around the sun, and in the spinning pattern of the galaxies through time and space. This most ancient of symbols shows the winding path we follow in life; departure from one level, return to another, ebb and flow, moving outwardly and then returning to a different level. It marks the journey of the soul, which many of us find too difficult by the direct route, preferring instead the more roundabout route of a spiral climb, as also represented in the form of the pyramid.

The spiral shows the way to the higher levels—and also to the lower ones. In Dante the seven levels of hell are reached through a dwindling spiral; to ascend you must first go to the very bottom. The spiral symbolizes the Mother Goddess as the weaver of human fates. In this aspect we have a parallel with the symbol of spider and spindle. The spiral also forms the labyrinth, the maze which we follow in order to get to the very center of our being and confront the Minotaur within ourselves. The traditional dragon or serpent would often sit at the center of such a spiral, guarding its very heart. We can find mazes such as these in the Neolithic art of Australia, and in European megaliths and burial mounds.

In ancient times, priests and priestesses divined the future by looking at the spiraling entrails of their sacrificial victims. In Kundalini yoga the serpent of tantra coiled itself around the base of the spine three and a half times, to be awakened through meditation and chanting, rising up through the energy centers of the body to either enlighten the seeker or drive him or her mad. In Turkey, the whirling dervishes use a spiral dance as the means of inspiring themselves to a higher level of awareness of God.

In the mystical Tree of Life, the Serpent of Wisdom coils up from the material plane of Malkuth to Kether, showing the order in which the paths are to be experienced by the Qabalist in order to attain a union with God.

On a practical level, the coins suggest how we each relate to issues such as work, income, savings, how we use money, and how we look after our physical well-being.

ACE OF COINS

We see Celeborn, husband of Galadriel, the Elf Lady of Lothlórien, sitting on his throne. On the back of it we see a spiral, symbol of earth energies. Celeborn was an Elf-lord, a prince of great fame—he was also called Celeborn the Wise. He shows the way to new openings through which our creative juices can begin to flow.

Tarot Meaning
A new doorway opening, leading to a greater opportunity in a work or material aspect.

TWO OF COINS

The Ents are at their Ent Moot, drinking their refreshing Ent-draughts. The Ents were responsible for the destruction of Saruman's tower Orthanc. They were very ancient creatures whose function was to shepherd the trees, and they lived in Fangorn Forest. Indeed, they had grown to resemble trees. They moved slowly, thought things over very carefully before acting, and didn't like to become involved in the disputes between the different groups in Middle-earth. They decided to attack Saruman because he cut trees in their forests to fuel his industrial activities and machinery.

Tarot Meaning
Moving on to do some work in another location. A shift in scenery.

THREE OF COINS

Bilbo Baggins is in his home in the Shire, where he is writing in the Red Book of Westmarch. The pages of the open book read "The road goes ever on and on." Around the room, we can see his many books. On the left bookshelf is the rune sign Algiz, which means protection. On the wall is a blank mirror, inviting us to look into it and see our own reflection. On the mantelpiece and around the room lie various boxes and caskets, probably containing some of the many artifacts Bilbo had obtained on his journeys. The clock on the table reads 12:15, although we are not sure whether that is after midnight or after noon. Twelve is a powerful magic number, representing good investments.

Tarot Meaning
Learning and developing new skills and abilities; a good investment of one's time and efforts.

FOUR OF COINS

The Great Tree of Lothlórien symbolizes the determination of the Free Peoples to survive against overwhelming odds. Lothlórien was the only place in Middle-earth where the golden mallorn trees grew, great trees with golden leaves and flowers and silver bark. The Elves made their homes in these trees. The Great Tree was where the Companions took counsel with Galadriel, Celeborn, and the Elves. Symbolically, the tree is the bridge between heaven and earth—its roots reach down into the underworld, while its branches extend up into the sky.

Tarot Meaning
Determining to get matters organized.

FIVE OF COINS

Unable to get across the Misty Mountains at the pass of Caradhras, the Companions stand outside the gateway to Moria. From the lake, the Watcher in the Water rears its tentacles to try to catch them. Gandalf tries to find the phrase that will open the doors. Above is written in runes (our translation from Tengwar), "Speak Friend and Enter." Off to the side is Bill the Pony, who ran away from the Watcher but survived. Next to Gandalf stands Boromir, in a Viking-like helmet, Legolas the Elf, armed with bow and arrows, and Gimli the Dwarf, armed with an ax. Aragorn sits on the ground with his sword drawn, and behind him are Frodo, Sam, Pippin, and Merry. Above the gateway are the symbols of the Dwarven Kingdom, the hammer and anvil and the crown; and the many-rayed star, symbol of the High Elves.

Tarot Meaning
Unforeseen challenges and expenses. Material obstacles and difficulties, and the need to find a way beyond them.

SIX OF COINS

A composite scene: Bilbo Baggins has found his way into Smaug's treasure hoard. In his hand he holds the Arkenstone, a gem of great brilliance and worth. Various other treasures, some in caskets, lie scattered around him. Smaug the dragon is shown in the entrance. After Smaug's death, various armies came from miles around to claim the treasure trove. The Arkenstone was especially prized by Thorin the Dwarf. Bilbo, wearing the One Ring, became invisible and smuggled the Arkenstone out to the besieging Elves and Men, in an attempt to secure a peaceful resolution of the conflict. This stone was later buried with Thorin.

Tarot Meaning
Good fortune and well-being. The need to share, but to do so with a sense of discrimination.

SEVEN OF COINS

The Company is trying to get across the Misty Mountains at the pass of Caradhras (Redhorn). But storms and avalanches drove them back, and they had to go through the Mines of Moria instead. Here Boromir, with his great strength, leads the party through the snow. Above them is the image of a septogram, a seven-pointed star, which shows fulfillment.

Tarot Meaning
Possibly very strong obstacles, but the need for perseverance in order to see the fulfillment of your projects. The need to continue, although other methods of achieving your objectives may need to be employed.

EIGHT OF COINS

Faramir is healing from injuries incurred during the battle for Minas Tirith. Kingsfoil, a healing herb, is dominant in the background; in the king's hands, it could counteract the Black Breath of the Ringwraiths and save many lives. The seven-pointed star stands on a staff with a golden point in the topmost angle proclaiming the power of healing and signifying completion. Above the characters, we see an eight-pointed figure, which represents the application of the intellect. The number eight is associated with Mercury, who rules over medicine, healing, science, and knowledge. At its center we see a marigold, symbol of the sun and its regenerative powers.

Tarot Meaning
The use of specialized knowledge in order to accomplish an objective. Here, knowledge is applied, whereas in the three of coins there is more of a sense of knowledge being gained and assimilated.

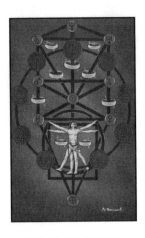

NINE OF COINS

The Tree of Life, with each of the Sephiroth showing an appropriate astrological association. The figure of a man with outstretched arms and legs is pictured forming a square within the parameters of his movement, thus showing the power of humanity to manifest the power of the spiritual directing forces of the universe. Around the limbs of the tree are the Nine Rings made for Mortal Men that Sauron captured from the Elves and that were linked to the One Ring. In the background looms the galaxy, with the outline of stars in the distance. The tree is radiant, and the man is the channel through which cosmic power is intended to express itself into this material plane. The Tree of Life is shown positioned within a 360 degree circle, representing spiritual protection of men and women under its branches.

Tarot Meaning
Recognition and acknowledgment for an accomplishment or completion of a task.

TEN OF COINS

Smaug is in his treasure trove, enjoying the glow that it gives off. A lust for gold is a weakness of dragons. In the background are ten spirals, this time connected up to each other in a manner resembling the diagrams of the international banking system, with all of the outer spirals (branches) linked up to the central one. The symbolic view is that of a central office pulling in from sub-offices. It suggests that perhaps Smaug has moved on to bigger and better things!

Tarot Meaning
Wealth and fortune, joint finances, and important investment decisions.

PAGE OF COINS

Glorfindel rides his white steed Asfaloth. He was a great lord in his own right, and the second most important Elf in Rivendell after Elrond. He met and protected Frodo and his companions on the way to Rivendell, and fought the Black Riders at the Ford of Loudwater.

Tarot Meaning
The desire to change your line of work, or to take on new responsibilities.

KNIGHT OF COINS

A Knight of Gondor is fully armed and on the alert. The White Tree of Gondor is emblazoned on his shield, with seven stars on its branches and a red rose beneath.

Tarot Meaning
A man who wants to develop his life in a specific direction.

QUEEN OF COINS

Pictured here is Lúthien Tinúviel, the Elf princess who was the most beautiful of all the children of Ilúvatar (God), and the ancestor of Aragorn and Arwen. Beren, a mortal Man, beheld Lúthien singing and dancing in the twilight, and named her Tinúviel, "nightingale." Lúthien defied her father to follow Beren and joined him on the quest of the Silmaril. She rescued Beren from the dungeons of Sauron, and together they cast down Morgoth the Great Enemy, and stole a Silmaril from his iron crown. But Beren was killed by a wolf, and Lúthien died of grief. She sang before the Valar in the Halls of the Dead, and the gods themselves were moved to pity. Then Ilúvatar gave Lúthien a choice: to return to life as an Elf, alone, or as a mortal—with Beren. She chose mortality. In the sky we see a dove, for peace; and a butterfly, for transformation. At her feet sit rabbits, symbolizing fertility. Above Lúthien's head are three interlaced Rings for the Elves, although they were forged long after her incarnation.

A biographical note: The story of Lúthien's dance was based on an actual incident in Tolkien's life, when his wife Edith danced for him in the twilit woods. Edith converted to Catholicism to marry Tolkien, just as Lúthien became mortal for the love of Beren; the names "Lúthien" and "Beren" are inscribed on the Tolkiens' gravestones.

Tarot Meaning
A woman who wants to manifest on the plane of earthly activity. She is ambitious and desires to see her plans realized.

KING OF COINS

Above the head of Treebeard, the leader of the Ents, rests a pair of antlers, with a wand or staff of rank held between their curling horns, showing him to be the leader of the pack. At Treebeard's feet grow several fly agaric, symbolic of initiation into the sacred mysteries. Treebeard was master of Fangorn Forest, a strange land inimical to outsiders.

Tarot Meaning

A man who has mastered the material conditions of life and is able to be supportive to others. He is concerned about his environment and is motivated into action to protect it.

V
Reading With
The Lord of the Rings Tarot Deck

The Lord of the Rings Tarot deck represents the marriage of two great traditions: the spiritual and mystical tradition of the tarot, and the world of legends, folklore, and fairy tales as epitomized by the fantasy writings of J. R. R. Tolkien, the greatest of such writers that this world has ever known.

This deck has been created along traditional tarot lines, and therefore consists of two sections: the Major Arcana and the Minor Arcana. The Major Arcana shows the 22 spiritual lessons for each one of us in this lifetime. They show us explanations as to how we can live more effective and fulfilling lives. The Minor Arcana represent 56 everyday life situations: times of conflict, joy, sharing, loss, success, failure, and so on.

In order to be able to use this deck to maximum advantage, I have included a few tips to help you. It would be helpful to have at least the basic meaning of each card firmly ingrained in your memory—nothing is so frustrating as having to look up each card meaning every time you read tarot cards.

MEDITATION WITH
THE LORD OF THE RINGS TAROT DECK

One of the beautiful aspects of working with this deck is that because Tolkien tapped into such a powerful realm of imagery, by laying out these cards and "imaging" yourself into their scenes you can enjoy a very experiential journey, rather than just using your tarot deck as a divinatory device that only comes out when you want to know the answer to a particular question.

You may wish to journey into Middle-earth in this way, and "meet" the characters there, such as Gandalf, Sam, Galadriel, the Lady Arwen. In so doing, you will enhance what the characters are able to do for you in the context of your own life.

In order to meet with these characters, pick out the relevant card which will act as the doorway, and, either while staring into the card in a relaxed way, or closing your eyes, imagine yourself as being a part of the scene.

The full technique is for you to lie down, or sit in your favorite chair, making sure that you are going to have enough time to be able to get into the meditation. You will probably need a good half an hour to start with. Later, as you progress, and the complexity and sophistication of your journeys increase, you may well find yourself needing more time. Breathe deeply, and count up to a hundred. Don't be in a rush to get there—in this realm, rushing will only slow you down.

Imagine yourself being surrounded by a green light, filtering in through the back of your neck, and filling your body. Then let yourself be transported into the scene you have selected, and "look around." See what you are wearing. Feel the texture of your clothes in this dimension. Feel what the ground is like under your feet. Let the scene come to life as it will, at its own pace. Let the character or characters begin to talk to you. They may take you somewhere, or show you something. They may even give you a gift. Look after it. What they show you may pertain to your past, your present situation, or even something which the future holds. Remember what your experience is, and when it has run its own natural course, let yourself return to normal waking consciousness and become more aware of your surrounding environment.

READING FOR YOURSELF

One of the simplest yet most effective of spreads to use for yourself is the Triadic Spread, so named after the ancient symbol of the Chosen Chief of the Druid Order. It shows—in a flash—aspects of past, present, and future. Unlike the Celtic Cross spread, which is more complex and can only be used for reading other people's cards, this spread is good for both oneself and others.

As you shuffle the deck, think about different aspects of your situation. Your question may be specific, perhaps about a particular problem, or it may be more general if you are interested in gaining a new perspective in your life. Let your thoughts flow, as it were, into the cards in your hands, and when you feel that the moment is ripe, stop and lay the cards out in the Triadic pattern, drawing the cards from the top of the deck and laying them face up in front of you. You can add extra cards to flow out from the first three, and as you do so you will gain further information from what you see in them.

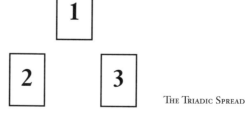

THE TRIADIC SPREAD

Reading For Other People

If you are reading for other people, remember that you have a particular responsibility. Many people still think that whatever is shown in the cards is their future, unchanging and carved in stone. The purpose of the tarot is to show us options which we may never have realized existed. It is an excellent medium of communication, but not something to let take over our lives. The tarot is all about friendship and good company; this is as important as the knowledge and power that are also attributed to the tarot. We will get from our tarot experiences precisely what we bring into them.

You will find these guidelines helpful when reading for others:

Keep the reading interactive. Let the querent—the person you are doing the reading for—ask questions. The reading should be a personal experience for them; not just a set of statements recited by rote which could apply to anyone.

Avoid negative predictions. It is one thing to feel that there may be obstacles ahead for your querent, but in this case use the cards to see how they can overcome these obstacles, rather than discouraging the querent with negative predictions.

Advise your querent in a common-sensical way. There has to be a practical element to your guidance.

Move as you wish between the cards, looking at past, present, and future. Look at aspects of their life such as home, family, hopes, fears, work, love, etc. Try and anticipate the querent's questions. What might they be interested in looking into?

Absorb the mood of the querent. Let yourself feel their fears, share their hopes.

When you feel that the querent needs a gentle push in the right direction, be encouraging, but don't be strident and try to make them do what you would do in their situation. We all have our own ways of dealing with the curve balls that life throws.

Be authentic. Believe in what you are saying, or predicting, or don't say or predict it. Be yourself. You don't have to be something out of a Hollywood film. Genuinely befriend the querent. You will be remembered positively in the years to come if you do this.

Avoid casting spells. Bring an element of your own charisma into the reading; that is a vital part of the sharing experience. But don't compound your querent's situation by bringing in any scary supernatural nonsense or heavy occultism. It doesn't lead to any good.

Avoid giving advice on legal matters and health issues. In these areas the cards are nowhere near as useful as the actual experts in those fields. A tarot reading is basically a philosophical review of one's life more than anything else.

Bring your reading into a story-like format, incorporating what you learn about your querent's life. Let yourself be able to picture it in your mind's eye. Nothing sounds as bad as a set of staccato, bullet-like statements delivered in a mechanistic fashion.

Plant positive seeds as you go along. Most predictions become self-fulfilling. Don't forget that the person sitting in front of you has power and potential, and therefore the ability to make incredible things happen. They are there with you having their cards read in order to be able to realize it.

The Gandalf Spread

This spread is in the form of the Elvish letter "G." This letter has special symbolic connotations, as it is the seventh letter of the English alphabet, and seven is the holy number of completion. For this reason, there are seven cards in the spread. The energy of Gandalf captured in this spread helps us to achieve a more active, effective role for ourselves in our lives.

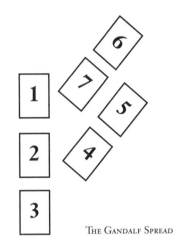

The Gandalf Spread

1. The present situation
2. The near future
3. The recent past
4. What is on the querent's mind
5. Hopes or anxieties
6. Opposing, contrary influences
7. Helpful, supportive influences

Taking your tarot pack in hand, pass the cards to the querent and ask him to shuffle. Get the querent to let his thoughts flow into the cards so that they may contain a true representation of his inner world; you might suggest that the querent breathe into the cards to help achieve this. When the querent hands the pack back to you, silently and from your inner center call upon Gandalf to be present; his image is comforting and a source of strength. If you feel tense, slow down by consciously breathing more deeply. The querent can join you in this exercise. After a few moments of deep, rhythmic breathing, lay the cards out in the Gandalf spread as shown.

SAMPLE READING USING THE GANDALF SPREAD

The cards fall into the spread as follows:

1. Ace of Wands
2. Three of Wands
3. Judgment
4. The World
5. The Queen of Coins
6. Nine of Coins
7. Ace of Swords

1. "Your present situation indicates a new initiative or activity which you are either recently involved in or are thinking about starting." This would vary depending on the person and their work. It might indicate a new business or investment, a new course of study, or transition from training to practice in a career or activity.

2. "The Three of Wands shows that you are ahead of your competitors, and that this is your main advantage. You are constantly keeping ahead with your innovative and explorative style. The implication is that you must not start slowing down now, because if you do those same people may well catch up and surpass you."

3. "Judgment represents your recent past, and refers to the major transformations you have been through. The influence of

this card could indicate several different lifestyles over the years, and, in its association with Pluto, attests to your fierce determination to win against the odds. Judgment also shows intense personal experiences that still affect you." As the reader, you might want to ask the querent what experiences the card may be referring to; let the querent let off some steam, and take you into his confidence; or if he wants to keep matters to himself, respect this as well.

4.   "The important issue on your mind seems to be connected with your worldly success, and the sense of self-esteem that accompanies success. There may be a big career breakthrough on the horizon, and the project you are working on may be your means to find and achieve this breakthrough."

5.   "Many of your hopes are bound up with a woman who is shown as the Queen of Coins. This woman represents someone who would like to develop the material and objective conditions of life. It could be someone that you know through work or business, or who shares your vision of what can be achieved through hard work and brain power."

6.   "An opposing influence is shown in the Nine of Coins, which betokens recognition that one has already gained. This may make it difficult for some people to take you seriously and respond to your offers." At the very least, the querent should not automatically assume that because he has had success in other realms that success will come easily in the area in question.

7.   "The Ace of Swords points to a major breakthrough coming about through a current project. Thus, your involvement is worthwhile, and you should proceed with confidence, noting the warnings—both implicit and explicit—that the cards have also given."

The Hobbit Spread

This spread is shaped like the letter H, which stands for Hobbit, but also represents the runic letter Hagal, meaning "hail."

1. The present situation
2. The querent's objective
3. Forces supporting the querent
4. Forces opposing the querent
5. The significance of the last twelve months
6. The forecast for the next twelve months
7. General overview, any other business

The Hobbit Spread

The Celtic Cross Spread

The Celtic Cross Spread is also good to use when you are reading for other people.

1. The querent's present position
2. Immediate sphere of influence on the querent
3. Querent's goal or destiny
4. Influence of distant past
5. Influence of recent past events
6. Future influences
7. The questioner's attitude in the present circumstances
8. Environmental factors; effect of other people on the querent
9. Inner emotions, hopes, fears, anxieties
10. Final outcome

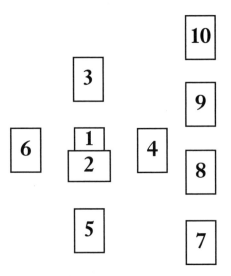

THE CELTIC CROSS SPREAD

Bibliography

By J. R. R. Tolkien

Farmer Giles of Ham. London: HarperCollins, 1949.

The History of Middle-Earth (Vol. 1-12), edited by Christopher Tolkien. London: HarperCollins, 1983-1996.

The Hobbit. London: HarperCollins, 1937, 1966.

The Lord of the Rings. London: HarperCollins, 1955, 1965.

The Silmarillion, edited by Christopher Tolkien. London: HarperCollins, 1977.

About Tolkien and his work

Humphrey Carpenter. *Tolkien: A Biography*. London: Grafton, 1977, 1992.

David Day. *A Tolkien Bestiary*. London: Mitchell Beazley, 1979.

David Day. *Tolkien: The Illustrated Encyclopedia*. New York: MacMillan and Company, 1991.

Peter Fenlon, et al. *Lords of Middle-earth (Vol. 1-3)*. Charlottesville, Virginia: Tolkien Enterprises, 1989.

Robert Foster. *The Complete Guide to Middle-earth: From The Hobbit to The Silmarillion*. New York: DelRey, 1978.

Robert Giddings and Elizabeth Holland. *The Shores of Middle-earth*. London: Junction Books, 1981.

Daniel Grotta. *A Biography of J. R. R. Tolkien: Architect of Middle-earth*. Philadelphia: Running Press, 1992.

Paul H. Kocher. *Master of Middle-earth: The Fiction of J. R. R. Tolkien*. Boston: Houghton Mifflin Company, 1972.

Ruth S. Noel. *The Mythology of Middle-earth*. Boston: Houghton Mifflin Company, 1977.

Barbara Strachey. *The Journeys of Frodo: An Atlas of J. R. R. Tolkien's The Lord of the Rings*. London: HarperCollins, 1981, 1992.

On symbolism and legends

Thomas Bulfinch. *The Golden Age of Myth and Legend*. London: Bracken, 1919, 1986.

Clara Erskine Clement. *Legendary and Mythological Art*. London: Bracken, 1994.

Barry Cunliffe. *The Celtic World*. New York: McGraw Hill, 1979.

H. R. Ellis Davidson. *Myths and Symbols in Pagan Europe*. Manchester, England: Manchester University Press, 1988.

The New Larousse Encyclopedia of Mythology. Hamlyn, 1993.

T. W. Rolleston. *Celtic Myths and Legends*. London: Bracken, 1986.

T. W. Rolleston. *The Illustrated Guide to Celtic Mythology*. London: Studio Editions, 1995.

Grafton E. Smith. *Evolution of the Dragon*. Albert Saifer, 1984.

On tarot

Terry Donaldson. *Dragon Tarot*. U.S. Games Systems, 1996.

Terry Donaldson. *Step-By-Step Tarot*. HarperCollins, 1995.

Terry and Evelyne Donaldson. *Principles of Tarot*. HarperCollins, 1996.

Amber Jayanti. *Living the Tarot*. Llewellyn, 1993.

Appendix

Tolkien Societies and Publications

Information on the very busy calendar of international Tolkien events can be obtained from any of these interconnected organizations.

Amon Hen
The Tolkien Society
contact via their website: http://www.tolkiensociety.org/

Mythlore and *Mythprint:* Journals of the Mythopoeic Society (a non-profit international literary and educational organization for the study, discussion, and enjoyment of fantasy and mythic literature)
The Mythopoeic Society
P.O. Box 6707
1008 N. Monterey
Altadena, CA 91003
website: http://home.earthlink/~emfarrell/mythsoc/mythsoc.html

The Tolkien Collector
Christina Scull, Editor
30 Talcott Road
Williamstown, MA 01267
A newsletter about collecting Tolkien's books.

Minas Tirith Evening Star
American Tolkien Society
P.O. Box 373
Highland, MI 48357-0373

Beyond Bree
Newsletter of American Mensa Tolkien Special Interest Group
Nancy Martsch, Editor
P.O. Box 55372
Sherman Oaks, CA 91413

About the Creators of
The Lord of the Rings Tarot

TERRY DONALDSON is a professional tarot reader and teacher, and is one of the leading representatives of the tarot in the world today. He is a founder and director of the London Tarot Centre, which offers a high level of training to individuals in the art and craft of tarot readership, astrology, and divinatory techniques. Terry is the author of two internationally-acclaimed books on tarot, *Step-By-Step Tarot* (Thorsons) and *Principles of Tarot* (with Evelyne Donaldson, published by Thorsons), both of which have been translated into Spanish, German, and Italian.

He is the co-creator of the mythological collectible card game Wyvern, and of the Dragon Tarot, which explores the mystical symbolism of the dragon and associated legends throughout history. Terry is currently at work on more projects inspired by Middle-earth symbolism.

For many years, Terry has traveled through Iran, Afghanistan, and India, studying under the direction of a number of masters and teachers in yoga, meditation, and tantra. His work is oriented toward self-development and empowerment, and it is in this spirit that he approaches the tarot. He is also a Master of the Kabbala School of Initiation.

Terry is a leading member of the Folk Lore Society and the Society of Authors. He is a former initiate of the Order of Bards, Ovates and Druids, and holds a First Class honors degree in economics from The London School of Economics. He has a daughter, Claudia.

Terry has designed both a special personalized training program and a correspondence course based on The Lord of the Rings Tarot. To learn more about these, please contact him through the London Tarot Centre (see page 268).

PETER PRACOWNIK is a leading artist of the Visionary School, and painted the cards in both Wyvern and the Dragon Tarot. There is a special sensitivity in Peter's pictures that emphasizes the force of nature counterpoised against the spiritual realms of experience. Peter has long had a special association with the Arthurian legends, the Merlin archetype, and the pre-Christian cultures of Northern Europe. He is an avid collector of ancient coins and artifacts.

Peter lives in the west country of England, the setting for the legends of the Piskies and Knockers of Cornwall, Tristan and Isolde, Lorna Doone, and King Arthur.

Peter's art has been shown in exhibitions in Europe and the United States. The artwork in The Lord of the Rings Tarot reflects Peter's own unique vision and interpretation of Tolkien's stories and characters.

Those interested in learning more about tarot training programs or receiving professional tarot readings may contact Terry Donaldson at:

> The London Tarot Centre
> 25 Gisburn Road
> Hornsey
> London N8 7BS
> England
>
> Telephone: (44) 181-340-3788
> Fax: (44) 181-348-8665